ASVAB

Study Guide: Mock Practice Tests

100s of practice questions, detailed answers, and high-scoring strategies for passing the Armed Service Vocational Aptitude Battery Exam

As part of this product you have also received FREE access to online tests that will help you to pass the Armed Forces selection tests:

To gain access, simply go to:

www.MyPsychometricTests.co.uk

Get more products for passing any test at:

www.How2Become.com

Orders: Please contact How2Become Ltd, Suite 14, 50 Churchill Square Business Centre, Kings Hill, Kent ME19 4YU.

You can order through Amazon.co.uk under ISBN: **9781912370207**, via the website www.How2Become.com or through Gardners.com.

ISBN: **9781912370207**

First published in 2018 by How2Become Ltd.

Typeset by Katie Noakes for How2Become Ltd.

Printed and bound by CPI Group (UK) Ltd, Croydon, CR0 4YY

Disclaimer

Every effort has been made to ensure that the information contained within this guide is accurate at the time of publication. How2Become Ltd is not responsible for anyone failing any part of any selection process as a result of the information contained within this guide. How2Become Ltd and their authors cannot accept any responsibility for any errors or omissions within this guide, however caused. No responsibility for loss or damage occasioned by any person acting, or refraining from action, as a result of the material in this publication can be accepted by How2Become Ltd.

The information within this guide does not represent the views of any third party service or organisation.

CONTENTS

INTRODUCTION

INTRODUCTION TO YOUR NEW GUIDE

Welcome to your new guide, *ASVAB Study Guide: Mock Practice Tests*.

Here at How2Become, we have done our utmost to provide a guide packed full of hundreds of sample testing questions. This guide will be invaluable to anyone who wishes to join the United States military.

Tasked with defence, the US military play a crucial role in the protection of the country. Joining the military in any type of role will require hard work and determination. The selection tests used within the US military are designed to assess whether potential candidates have the 'ability' to meet the demanding nature of life within the service.

The purpose of this book is to guide you through the psychometric tests used to join the United States military. It has been written with the intention of bettering your scores and improving your overall performance. Generally, the higher scores you achieve during the assessment, the more job opportunities you will have at your disposal. We guarantee you a professional guide, which will help you to fully grasp psychometric tests and assist you during your preparation period.

You will find that the more practice you undertake in the build up to your test, the better you will perform on the day. Each testing chapter assesses similar skills and qualities, and therefore practising all of the questions in this guide can only better your chances of success.

STRUCTURE OF THE GUIDE

In order to make the most out of your guide, we have formatted this book in a simple and clear structure, detailing all of the information and practice you will need if you wish to be successful.

The guide is broken up into nine key sub-sections, each relating to the different areas of the ASVAB process.

- General Science;
- Arithmetic Reasoning;
- Word Knowledge;
- Paragraph Comprehension;
- Mathematics Knowledge;
- Electronics Information;
- Auto and Shop Information;
- Mechanical Comprehension;
- Assembling Objects.

We suggest that you begin with the testing section that you are applying for, and then if you wish to practice more questions, you can work through the rest of the guide. The questions are of similar style, so practising them all will only improve the 'essential' skills needed to successfully pass the selection process.

Good luck and best wishes.

The How2Become Team

DETAILS ABOUT THE ASVAB

ABOUT THE ASVAB

To enlist in the US Armed Forces requires a high level of commitment, professionalism and skill. The Armed Services Vocational Aptitude Battery (ASVAB) is used to screen applicants to ensure that they measure up to the high standards that are required.

A career in the US Armed Forces comes with a great deal of responsibility, commitment and integrity. It provides many career opportunities and is lucrative in terms of prospects, potential and earnings. That is why it is important that the US Armed Forces employ people who show strong levels of enthusiasm and skill, in order to maintain a great level of service and professionalism.

Amidst the application process, you will be required to undergo a series of psychometric tests. These assessments have been used in the US Armed Forces recruitment process for many years, and are used to primarily assess a candidate's suitability for specific job roles. Potential candidates need to understand the integrity and nature of the job, and be able to demonstrate the 'core competencies' to a high standard, in order to fulfil and meet the challenging criteria of life in the US military.

You will be assessed by undergoing a series of tests which illustrate how well you can perform specified tasks – tasks that test similar skills to the ones you will have to demonstrate in a real life situation. The selection processes will vary depending on whether you are applying for a position in the Army, the Navy, Coast Guard, Air Force, or the Marine Corps, so it is important that you know what process you will be involved with, in order to successfully complete the psychometric stages of the assessment.

Each test used in the selection process is used for a particular reason. The level of difficulty for each test will also vary depending on the job position for which you are applying. Therefore it is vital that you improve your skills and performance by preparing as much as you can prior to your assessment.

WHAT TEST ARE YOU TAKING?

The ASVAB comes in four different versions. The version that you will be required to undertake will very much depend on who you are applying to, and why you are taking it.

Whether you are in high school and are required to take the ASVAB as part of the Careers Exploration Program, or enlisting to join the Armed Forces by applying to MEPS, the content of the ASVAB will remain the same.

Below we have categorized the different types of version for the ASVAB, along with key information about the purpose and format of the assessment:

- **ENLISTMENT**

The ASVAB will usually be computer-based and will be provided by military recruiters at MEPS (Military Entrance Processing Stations). This will be used to determine what military opportunities you have at your disposal.

- **ENGLISH SCREENING TEST (EST)**

The ASVAB will be computer-based and will be provided by a military recruiter to quickly screen a candidate. This acts as a mini-assessment, whereby it is used to determine whether a person is likely to obtain qualifying test scores.

- **ARMED FORCES CLASSIFICATION TEST (AFCT)**

The ASVAB will be computer-based and will be provided by educational centers to people already in the military. This is usually done if a person wants to retrain for a different job in military.

- **STUDENT**

The ASVAB will be paper-based and is given to students in the junior or senior years at high school. This is used as part of an educational program to decipher whether a career in the Armed Forces is suitable.

THE ASVAB TESTS

There are ten subtests which form the ASVAB assessment. The Auto & Shop Information test is split into two halves. The paper format of the assessment will only consist of nine subtests.

PLEASE NOTE: students will not be required to sit the Assembling Objects subtest.

Subtest	Computer version	Paper version	Content
General Science (GS)	16 questions 8 minutes	25 questions 11 minutes	General biological and physical principles
Arithmetic Reasoning (AR)	16 questions 39 minutes	30 questions 36 minutes	Word problems requiring high school knowledge
Word Knowledge (WK)	16 questions 8 minutes	35 questions 11 minutes	Correct word meaning
Paragraph Comprehension (PC)	11 questions 22 minutes	15 questions 13 minutes	Read a passage and answer questions
Mathematics Knowledge (MK)	16 questions 20 minutes	25 questions 24 minutes	High school mathematical knowledge
Electronics Information (EI)	16 questions 8 minutes	20 questions 9 minutes	General electronic principles
Auto & Shop Information (AS)	22 questions 13 minutes	25 questions 11 minutes	Knowledge of tools and automobiles
Mechanical Comprehension (MC)	16 questions 20 minutes	25 questions 19 minutes	Basic mechanical knowledge
Assembling Objects (AO)	16 questions 15 minutes	25 questions 15 minutes	Spatial orientation

UNDERSTANDING ASVAB SCORES

Standard Scores are reported for each individual subtest of the ASVAB. One of the biggest things to concentrate on is your AFQT (Armed Forces Qualification Test) score.

Your AFQT will be formed using four of the subtest scores:

- Arithmetic Reasoning;

- Mathematics Knowledge;

- Word Knowledge;

- Paragraph Comprehension.

Different fields in the US military will require different test scores. The other subtest scores are used to narrow down your choices of jobs within that field.

Below we have provided you with a simple breakdown of what each service branch requires with regards to AFQT scores.

Service	AFQT score
Army	31
Navy	35
Marines	32
Air Force	36
Coast Guard	40

PLEASE NOTE: the minimum test scores are liable to change without notice.

WHERE TO TAKE THE ASVAB

With regards to whereabouts you take the ASVAB, will depend on the reasoning for taking it.

If you are a high school student, you will take the assessment at your high school.

If you are enlisting for the US military, you will be required to attend the nearest Military Entrance Processing Station (MEPs) or Military Entrance Test (MET) site.

For a full breakdown of MEPs ASVAB testing location, please see **APPENDIX A**.

HOW LONG ARE THE ASVAB RESULTS VALID FOR?

The ASVAB results are valid for 2 years. This is true so long as you are not currently in the military.

PREPARATION FOR THE ASVAB

The best way to prepare for the ASVAB is to undergo in-depth practice material.

Academic knowledge is crucial to help you obtain high scores in the following areas:

- Mathematics;

- English;

- Science.

By improving your knowledge in the above areas, you will be far more competent in each of the subtests of the ASVAB.

The following are general tips to help you make the most out of your preparation time:

- Prepare well in advance of your assessment.

- Learn what to expect on the day of your ASVAB.

- Familiarize yourself with each subtest of the ASVAB.

- Undergo sample questions in each subtest of the ASVAB.

- Learn what version of the ASVAB you are taking.

- Keep in mind the reason you are taking the ASVAB. What are your dreams in relation to your career?

- Keep an eye on the time. Don't spend too long on one question.

- If you are struggling to work out the answer, try to eliminate answer options.

THE CAT-ASVAB

The CAT-ASVAB is a computer adaptive test. It is an automated test which uses test administration to display test scores, record answers, computes your AFQT score and allows you to be flexible with your time.

This test is often used at Military Entrance Processing Stations (MEPs) for enlistment purposes.

Below we have outlined some of the key advantages and disadvantages of using the CAT-ASVAB.

Advantages	Disadvantages
• Adapts difficulty based on your level of skill and proficiency.	• You can't skip questions and come back to them.
• Contains fewer questions compared to the paper version.	• You can't change your answers.
• It's impossible to record answers in the wrong place.	• You have to answer the questions in the order that they appear.
• You get your scores immediately.	• You can't go back at the end of the test and check your answers.

THE P&P-ASVAB

The P&P-ASVAB is a pen and paper version of the ASVAB. This is one of the ways in which you might be assessed to join the US military.

Below we have outlined some of the key advantages and disadvantages of using the P&P-ASVAB.

Advantages	Disadvantages
• You can skip through questions you're unsure of and come back to them.	• Level of difficulty is set.
	• You have to wait for scores.
• You can make notes.	• You could mark the wrong answer box, meaning you will lose marks.

RETAKING THE ASVAB

If you fail the ASVAB, that means you have failed to score 10 or more in the AFQT. The AFQT comprises of four subtests:

- Arithmetic Reasoning;

- Word Knowledge;

- Paragraph Comprehension;

- Mathematics Knowledge.

If you've sat the ASVAB once, and that includes taking it at high school level, you will be able to resit the ASVAB one month after your last attempt.

If you fail to pass your second retest, you will have to wait at least 6 months before applying again.

Each US military service has its own rules and regulations regarding resits.

US ARMY

The US Army will allow a candidate to resit the ASVAB if one of the following applies:

- If the previous ASVAB test has expired;

- In the event that a candidate, through no fault of their own, is unable to complete the test;

- If the candidate failed to achieve an AFQT score to qualify for enlistment.

US NAVY

The US Navy will allow a candidate to resit the ASVAB if one of the following applies:

- If the previous ASVAB test has expired;

- If the candidate failed to achieve an AFQT score to qualify for enlistment.

US AIR FORCE

The US Air Force uses a retest of the ASVAB if a candidate wants to improve on their ASVAB scores to increase their job opportunities. An interview will be required prior to the ASVAB and must be approved by the recruiting flight clief.

The US Air Force also use the following policies:

- The Air Force does not allow retesting if they've enlisted in the Delayed Entry Program (DEP);

- The Air Force allows retesting of candidates who are not holding a job area reservation and/or who are not enlisted in DEP, but have already qualifying test scores;

- Authorized retesting if line scores limit the ability to match the Air Force skill with their qualifications.

US MARINE CORPS

The US Marine Corps will allow a candidate to resit the ASVAB if one of the following applies:

- If the previous ASVAB test has expired;

- If the initial scores don't reflect true capability and skill.

US COAST GUARD

The US Coast Guard will allow a candidate to resit the ASVAB if one of the following applies:

- If six months has elapsed since their last test;

- If the candidate wants to increase their test scores to qualify for particular enlistment opportunities;

- The recruiting center may authorize retests after one month has passed after ASVAB.

GENERAL SCIENCE

This is often described as one of the most difficult subtests in the ASVAB. The fact that you will be required to memorize factual and statistical information puts great pressure on you.

During this section of your Armed Forces assessment, the number of questions and the duration you have will depend on whether you are sitting the paper-based or computer-based version.

Subtest	Computer version	Paper version	Content
General Science (GS)	16 questions 8 minutes	25 questions 11 minutes	General biological and physical principles

PLEASE NOTE: the General Science (GS) section has **NO** impact on your Armed Forces Qualification Test (AFQT) score. However, don't take this as an opportunity to relax.

The score for this subtest will be used to calculate military composite scores for job qualification basis.

Use this chapter as a mini Science lesson to recap on your general Science knowledge. Below we have outlined the key areas that you should be focusing on:

CELLS	THE ANIMAL KINGDOM	PLANTS	DISEASES
PHOTOSYNTHESIS	RESPIRATION	THE HUMAN BODY	HORMONES
REPRODUCTION	GENETIC INHERITANCE	EVOLUTION	ECO-SYSTEMS
ATMOSPHERE	ATOMS	PERIODIC TABLE	STATES OF MATTER
MOLECULES	REACTION	ENERGY	ELECTRICITY
TEMPERATURE	MATERIALS	FORCES	WAVES
THE SOLAR SYSTEM	EXPANDING UNIVERSE	MAGNETISM	MATERIALS

Types of Science

Agriculture	The cultivation and breeding of plants, animals and fungi.
Archaeology	The study of human activity by recovering and analysing material/environment.
Astronomy	The study of celestial objects and phenomena.
Botany	The study of plant life – a branch of biology.
Chemistry	The study of composition, behaviour, properties, and reactions of matter.
Ecology	A branch of biology which studies interactions amongst organisms and their environment.
Entomology	A branch of zoology, entomology is the study of insects.
Genealogy	The study of families and heritage.
Genetics	The study of genes, genetic variations and heredity in organisms.
Geology	A study of Earth's surface, rocks, and the processes of change over time.
Ichthyology	A branch of zoology, ichthyology is the study of fish.
Meteorology	This is a study of weather forecasting, which looks at atmospheric chemistry and physics.
Paleontology	The study of fossils, animals and plants.
Physics	The study of force, energy, mechanics, waves and the physical universe.
Zoology	The study of the animal kingdom.

Units of Measurements

Length	Liquid Volume	Mass
Millimeter (mm)	Milliliter (mL)	Milligram (mg)
Centimeter (cm)	Centiliter (cL)	Centigram (cg)
Meter (m)	Liter (L)	Gram (g)
Kilometer (km)	Kiloliter (kL)	Kilogram (kg)

Metric System

Milli	One-thousandth (0.001)
Centi	One-hundredth (0.01)
Deci	One-tenth (0.1)
Deca	10
Hecto	100
Kilo	1,000
Mega	1,000,000

Temperatures

Fahrenheit (°F)	Fahrenheit is the most common temperature used in the United States. Water freezes at 32°F and boils at approximately 212°F.
Celsius (Centigrade) (°C)	This is the metric temperature used wordwide. Water freezes at 0°C and boils at 100°C.
Kelvin (K)	Scientists believe that the coldest temperature Earth can reach is -273.15°C. At this temperature it would stop molecular motion. This is called **absolute zero**. Water freezes at 273.15K and boils at 373.15K.

<u>To convert Fahrenheit to Celsius:</u>

$$C = \frac{5}{9}(F - 32)$$

<u>To convert Celsius to Fahrenheit:</u>

$$F = \frac{9}{5}\,C + 32$$

<u>To get the temperature in the Kevin scale:</u>

- Add 273.15 degrees to the Celsius temperature.

$$K = C + 273.15$$

- To convert from Kelvins to degrees, you will need to do the opposite. So, subtract 273.15 from the Kelvin temperature.

Human Body System	
Central Nervous System	The central nervous system receives, processes and responds to physical stimuli. The components of the body that make up the central nervous system are the brain, spinal cord and nerves.
Circulatory System	The circulatory system delivers oxygenated blood from the heart to the rest of the body. It returns the blood to the heart to be oxygenated again. The components of the body that make up the circulatory system are the heart, blood and blood vessels.
Digestive System	The digestive system breaks down food particles which allows your body to absorb and process them into energy and eliminates the waste. The components of the body that make up the digestive system are the stomach, intestines, mouth, esophagus, rectum and anus.
Muscoskeletal System	The muscoskeletal system allows bones to support the body, muscles and organs. It allows the joints to move, and muscles to work. The components of the body that make up the muscoskeletal system are the bones, joints and muscles.
Respiratory System	The respiratory system allows the body to inhale air and use the oxygen to release energy. The components of the body that make up the respiratory system are the nose, nasal cavity, trachea, lungs and the blood.

Cell Structure

Nucleus	The nucleus contains general materials which allows control of a cell's activity.
Cytoplasm	Cytoplasm is composed mainly of water, which can be found inside the cell membrane and outside the nucleus. The majority of chemical processes take place here which is controlled by enzymes.
Cell membrane	The cell membrane holds the cell together. It controls the movement of substances in and out of the cell.
Mitochondria	This is where most energy is released by respiration.
Ribosomes	This is where protein synthesis happens.

Cell Processes

Metabolism	This is the chemical process that occurs within cells in order to maintain life.
Osmosis	This is a process whereby water moves through cell membranes.
Phagocytosis	This is the process by which living cells ingest or engulf other cell particles. This is either done to destroy it, feed it or to learn from it.
Photosynthesis	Photosynthesis is the process used by plants and organisms to convert light into chemical energy. Plants therefore are able to make their own food with the use of sunlight.
Cellular Respiration	This is the process whereby food is broken down and used to produce energy.

Animal and Plant Cells

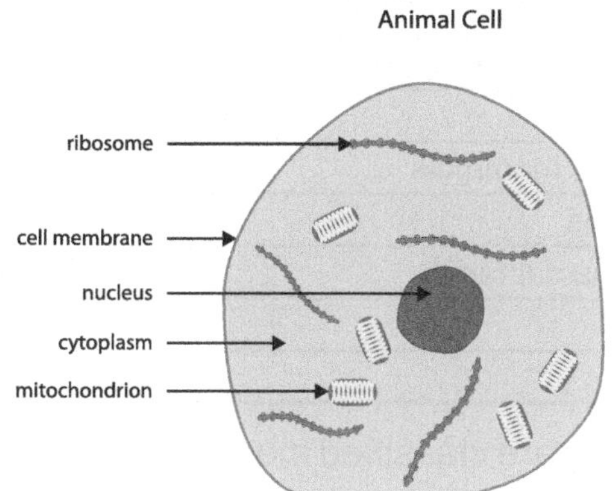

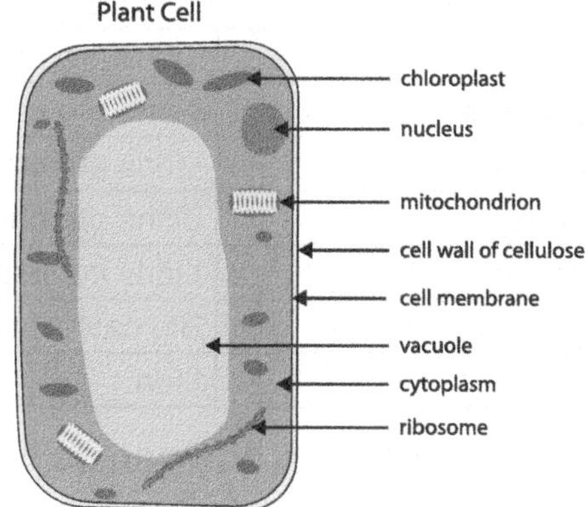

Animal Classification

Carnivores	An animal that feeds on other animals. Canivore means "meat eater".
Herbivores	A herbivore is an animal that eats plants.
Omnivores	An animal or person that eats both meat and plants.

Animal Classification

Let's take a look at how lions are classified more specifically:

Kingdom	Lions are part of the animal kingdom.
Phylum	Lions are vertebrates.
Class	Lions are classed as mammals.
Order	Lions are canivorous.
Family	Lions come from the cat family.
Genus	Big cats.
Species	Lion.

Let's take a look at how gentoo penguins are classified more specifically:

Kingdom	Gentoo penguins are part of the animal kingdom.
Phylum	Gentoo penguins are chordata.
Class	Gentoo penguins are classed as aves.
Order	Gentoo penguins are sphenisciformes.
Family	Gentoo penguins come from spheniscidae.
Genus	Penguins.
Species	Gentoo penguin.

The Different Kingdoms

Animals	The Animal Kingdom consists of more than one million different types of species. Animals don't have wall cells, chlophyll or the ability to photosynthesise. Members of the animal kingdom have the ability to move.
Plants	The plant kingdom includes organisms that do not move and don't have a nervous or sensory system. There are more than 250,000 species that belong to this category.
Monerans	Monerans inclue bacteria and cyanobacteria. They are one-celled organisms that do not contain a nucleus. There are more than 10,000 species of monerans.
Protists	Protists include one-celled organisms that do not contain a nucleus. There are over 250,000 species that belong to this category.
Fungi	Fungi contains cell walls made up of carbohyrdrates calle chitin. There are over 100,000 species that belong to this category.

Periodic Table

1	2	3	4	5	6	7	8	9	10	11	12	13	14	15	16	17	18
1 **H** Hydrogen																	2 **He** Helium
3 **Li** Lithium	4 **Be** Beryllium											5 **B** Boron	6 **C** Carbon	7 **N** Nitrogen	8 **O** Oxygen	9 **F** Fluorine	10 **Ne** Neon
11 **Na** Sodium	12 **Mg** Magnesium											13 **Al** Aluminium	14 **Si** Silicon	15 **P** Phosphorus	16 **S** Sulfur	17 **Cl** Chlorine	18 **Ar** Argon
19 **K** Potassium	20 **Ca** Calcium	21 **Sc** Scandium	22 **Ti** Titanium	23 **V** Vanadium	24 **Cr** Chromium	25 **Mn** Manganese	26 **Fe** Iron	27 **Co** Cobalt	28 **Ni** Nickel	29 **Cu** Copper	30 **Zn** Zinc	31 **Ga** Gallium	32 **Ge** Germanium	33 **As** Arsenic	34 **Se** Selenium	35 **Br** Bromine	36 **Kr** Krypton
37 **Rb** Rubidium	38 **Sr** Strontium	39 **Y** Yttrium	40 **Zr** Zirconium	41 **Nb** Niobium	42 **Mo** Molybdenum	43 **Tc** Technetium	44 **Ru** Ruthenium	45 **Rh** Rhodium	46 **Pd** Palladium	47 **Ag** Silver	48 **Cd** Cadmium	49 **In** Indium	50 **Sn** Tin	51 **Sb** Antimony	52 **Te** Tellurium	53 **I** Iodine	54 **Xe** Xenon
55 **Cs** Caesium	56 **Ba** Barium	57 **La*** Lanthanum	72 **Hf** Hafnium	73 **Ta** Tantalum	74 **W** Tungsten	75 **Re** Rhenium	76 **Os** Osmium	77 **Ir** Iridium	78 **Pt** Platinum	79 **Au** Gold	80 **Hg** Mercury	81 **Tl** Thallium	82 **Pb** Lead	83 **Bi** Bismuth	84 **Po** Polonium	85 **At** Astatine	86 **Rn** Radon
87 **Fr** Francium	88 **Ra** Radium	89 **Ac**** Actinium	104 **Rf** Rutherfordium	105 **Db** Dubnium	106 **Sg** Seaborgium	107 **Bh** Bohrium	108 **Hs** Hassium	109 **Mt** Meitnerium	110 **Ds** Darmstadtium	111 **Rg** Roentgenium	112 **Cn** Copernicium	113 **Uut** Ununtrium	114 **Fl** Flerovium	115 **Uup** Ununpentium	116 **Lv** Livermorium	117 **Uus** Ununseptium	118 **Uuo** Ununoctium

	58 **Ce** Cerium	59 **Pr** Praseodymium	60 **Nd** Neodymium	61 **Pm** Promethium	62 **Sm** Samarium	63 **Eu** Europium	64 **Gd** Gadolinium	65 **Tb** Terbium	66 **Dy** Dysprosium	67 **Ho** Holmium	68 **Er** Erbium	69 **Tm** Thulium	70 **Yb** Ytterbium	71 **Lu** Lutetium
**	90 **Th** Thorium	91 **Pa** Protactinium	92 **U** Uranium	93 **Np** Neptunium	94 **Pu** Plutonium	95 **Am** Americium	96 **Cm** Curium	97 **Bk** Berkelium	98 **Cf** Californium	99 **Es** Einsteinium	100 **Fm** Fermium	101 **Md** Mendelevium	102 **No** Nobelium	103 **Lr** Lawrencium

- Nonmetals
- Alkali metals
- Post-transition metals
- Noble gases
- Transition metals
- Lanthanides
- Metalloids
- Unknown
- Alkaline earth metals
- Actinides
- Halogens

Planets and Moons

Planet	Moons
Mercury	0
Venus	0
Earth	1
Mars	2 small satellites
Jupiter	63
Saturn	61
Uranus	27
Neptune	13
Pluto (dwarf planet)	3

Meteors, Comets, and Asteroids

Meteoroid	A meteoroid is a small rocky or metallic object in outer space. These are significantly smaller than asteroids.
Comet	A celestial object consisting of ice and dust. When near the sun, a tail of gas and dust particles points away from the sun.
Asteroid	A small rocky object orbiting the sun. An asteroid is a very small planet that moves around the sun between the planets Mars and Jupiter.

Earth's Atmosphere

Troposphere	The lowest region of the atmosphere.
Stratosphere	This is the second major layer of the Earth's atmosphere.
Mesosphere	This is directly under the stratosphere. The temperature decreases as altitude increases.
Ionosphere	This is the ionized part of the Earth's upper atmosphere.
Thermosphere	"Thermo" means heat. The temperature in this layer can reach a staggering 4,500 degrees Fahrenheit.
Exosphere	This is the uppermost region. This gradually fades into space. "Exo" means outside. It is the very edge of our atmosphere.

Clouds

Cloud Type	Description	What It Means
Cirrus	Thin, high clouds	Indicate rain or snow
Cumulus	White, puffy clouds	Fair weather. When they gather, they cause heavy rain
Stratus	Flat, low-hanging clouds	If close to the ground, may cause drizzle

GENERAL SCIENCE

QUICK TIPS

- Recap your knowledge with regards to basic scientific principles. Your knowledge should be at a high school level.

- Pay close attention to areas such as ecology, biology, astronomy, anatomy and geology.

- If you don't know the answer, take an educated guess. You can eliminate some of the options you know to be incorrect.

- Keep an eye on the time. Remember you only have 11 minutes to answer all 25 questions for the paper-version of the ASVAB (8 minutes to answer 16 questions on the computer-version). That works out to be around 26 seconds per question!

- If you don't know the answer, and cannot take an educated guess, leave it, and come back to it at the end if you have time.

- As with any test, it is important to undergo in-depth revision. The only way to enhance your knowledge is to revise Science. Break up your revision time using a timetable. Focus on the areas that you are not so confident with.

GENERAL SCIENCE PRACTICE QUESTIONS

QUESTION 1

The control center is often referred to as...

A. Cell membrane.

B. Cell nucleus.

C. Plasma membrane.

D. Chloroplasts.

QUESTION 2

What is the process called when one tectonic plate slides under another?

A. Abduction.

B. Inversion.

C. Subduction.

D. Orogenesis.

QUESTION 3

How many miles (approximately) does the troposphere extend above Earth?

A. 30 miles.

B. 50 miles.

C. 12 miles.

D. 2 miles.

QUESTION 4

If the temperature in Fahrenheit is 320°, what would the temperature in Celsius be?

A. 100°C.

B. 640°C.

C. 70°C.

D. 160°C.

QUESTION 5

Which body system most resembles the immune system?

A. Muscular system.

B. Respiratory system.

C. Digestive system.

D. Lymphatic system.

QUESTION 6

When is a comet's tail visible?

A. When the comet is close to the sun.

B. When the comet passes Jupiter.

C. When the rock and heat collide.

D. When the comet orbits the Earth.

QUESTION 7

What is the best definition of chlorophyll?

A. The ability to conduct photosynthesis.

B. An organic compound with the formula $CHCl_3$.

C. The material within a living cell.

D. A chemical that helps plants to create food using sunlight.

QUESTION 8

Taxonomy is mostly associated with which famous botanist?

A. Leonardo da Vinci.

B. Carl Linnaeus.

C. Gregor Mendel.

D. James Edward Smith.

QUESTION 9

When sound travels, when would the waves travel the fastest?

A. In a medium that is most dense.

B. In a medium that is less dense.

C. In a medium that is electronically charged.

D. In a medium that conducts heat.

QUESTION 10

What is the genus species of a horse?

A. Canis.

B. Danaus plexippus.

C. Acinonyx.

D. Equus.

ANSWERS TO GENERAL SCIENCE PRACTICE QUESTIONS

Q1. B. Cell nucleus.

Q2. C. Subduction.

Q3. C. 12 miles.

Q4. D. 160°C.

Q5. D. Lymphatic system.

Q6. A. When the comet is close to the sun.

Q7. D. A chemical that helps plants create food using sunlight.

Q8. B. Carl Linnaeus.

Q9. B. In a medium that is less dense.

Q10. D. Equus.

Now move on to the Arithmetic Reasoning subtest of the ASVAB.

ARITHMETIC REASONING

The Arithmetic Reasoning section of the ASVAB requires you to use mathematical principles in relation to the real world.

During this section of your Armed Forces assessment, the number of questions and the duration you have for this section will depend on whether you are sitting the paper-based or computer-based version.

Subtest	Computer version	Paper version	Content
Arithmetic Reasoning (AR)	16 questions 39 minutes	30 questions 36 minutes	Word problems requiring high school knowledge

PLEASE NOTE: the Arithmetic Reasoning (AR) section **DOES** have an impact on your Armed Forces Qualification Test (AFQT) score. Be sure to improve your high school math knowledge.

The score for this subtest will be used along with three other subtests to determine your AFQT score.

Use this chapter as a mini arithmetic lesson to recap on your general Mathematics knowledge. Below we have outlined the key areas that you should be focusing on:

ADD	SUBTRACT	MULTIPLY	DIVIDE
PERCENTAGES	DECIMALS	FRACTIONS	RATIO
PROPORTION	INTEREST	MONEY	SPEED
DISTANCE	TIME	MEASURES	PROBABILITY
STATISTICS	GEOMETRY	UNITS	INTEGERS
PRIME	SQUARED	MULTIPLES	FACTORS
ALGEBRA	SEQUENCES	WHOLE NUMBERS	PROBLEM SOLVING

The Arithmetic Reasoning section of the ASVAB will consist of math word problems. These questions will look very different to the questions in the Mathematical Knowledge (MK) subtest.

The key to preparing for Arithmetic Reasoning is to understand that there are two vital parts to work out an answer:

- The arithmetic;

- The reasoning.

The arithmetic is the part where you will have to perform mathematical operations. The reasoning part is where you will have to figure out what numbers to use in your calculations.

Types of Arithmetic

For a full breakdown of different types of arithmetic and basic mathematical calculations, go to the chapter 'Mathematics Knowledge', which can be found on page 79.

From here, you will be provided information on the following:

- Mathematics terminology;

- Order of operations;

- Integers;

- Inequalities;

- Fractions, decimals and percentages;

- Find x% of y;

- Expressing x as a percentage of y;

- Rounding up and rounding down;

- Multiples;

- Prime numbers;

- Percentage increase and percentage decrease;

- Ratios and proportions;

- Angles;

- 2D and 3D shapes;

- Algebra.

ARITHMETIC REASONING

QUICK TIPS

- Recap your knowledge with regards to basic mental arithmetic. Recap topics such as addition, subtraction and multiplication etc. Other areas that should be revised can be found on page 40.

- When you've answered the question consider whether your answer is probable. Does it actually answer the question? Does it seem realistic?

- If you don't know the answer, take an educated guess. You can eliminate some of the options you know to be incorrect.

- Keep an eye on the time. Remember you only have 36 minutes to answer all 30 questions for the paper-version of the ASVAB (39 minutes to answer 16 questions on the computer-version). That works out to be around 70 seconds per question!

- If you don't know the answer, leave it, and come back to it at the end if you have time.

- As with any test, it is important to undergo in-depth revision. The only way to enhance your knowledge is to revise Mental Arithmetic. Break up your revision time using a timetable. Focus on the areas that you are not so confident with.

ARITHMETIC REASONING
PRACTICE QUESTIONS

QUESTION 1

The cost of 22 books is $80.30. What is the average cost per book?

A. $7.10

B. $4.35

C. $5.50

D. $3.65

QUESTION 2

Sandy buys a coat for $25.99, a new pair of shoes for $19.98 and a new handbag which costs $25.00. How much change will Sandy receive if she hands over $80.00?

A. $9.03

B. $10.00

C. $6.05

D. $5.90

QUESTION 3

A school trip uses a minibus to go to a museum. The price of the minibus is calculated per kilometer. Each kilometer is $1.86, and they need to travel 45 kilometers in total. If 9 people were to split the cost equally, how much will each person pay?

A. $6.25

B. $10.50

C. $8.50

D. $9.30

QUESTION 4

On a school trip at least 1 teacher is needed for every 8 students. Work out the minimum number of teachers needed for 138 students.

A. 16

B. 17

C. 18

D. 19

QUESTION 5

During the day, the temperature reached a high of 85 degrees. That night, the temperature plummeted to a low of -10 degrees. What was the average temperature?

A. 40 degrees.

B. 39 degrees.

C. 37.5 degrees.

D. 35 degrees.

QUESTION 6

What would it cost to buy floor tiles for a room 12 feet wide and 15 feet long, if tiles cost $11.62 per square yard?

A. $220.17

B. $232.40

C. $248.62

D. $249.37

QUESTION 7

A traveller visits three cities, driving in a triangular route. He first drives from city A to B, 25 kilometers away, in 1 hour. He then drives from B to C, 20 kilometers away, in 30 minutes. Finally the traveller drives from C to A, 75 kilometers away, in 1 hour and 30 minutes.

Calculate the traveller's average speed.

A. 40 kilometers.

B. 35 kilometers.

C. 70 kilometers.

D. 65 kilometers.

QUESTION 8

Rachel works out that her flight will travel at a speed of 1,200km/h for 3 hours in order to arrive at her destination. If the flight was to cover the same distance but in a time of 1 hour and 30 minutes, the plane must travel at what speed (km/h)?

A. 80km/h.

B. 600km/h.

C. 60km/h.

D. 800km/h.

QUESTION 9

What is the width of a rectangular building with a perimeter of 66 meters and a length of 18 meters?

A. 15 meters.

B. 18 meters.

C. 22 meters.

D. 10 meters.

QUESTION 10

What is the price of an item that initially cost $600 after successive discounts of 15% and 20%?

A. $450

B. $330

C. $408

D. $512

ANSWERS TO ARITHMETIC REASONING PRACTICE QUESTIONS

Q1. D. $3.65

Q2. A. $9.03

Q3. D. $9.30

Q4. C. 18

Q5. C. 37.5 degrees.

Q6. B. $232.40

Q7. A. 40 kilometers.

Q8. D. 800km/h.

Q9. A. 15 meters.

Q10. C. $408

Now move on to the Word Knowledge subtest of the ASVAB.

WORD KNOWLEDGE

The Word Knowledge section of the ASVAB requires you to differentiate between words based on spelling, and their meaning.

During this section of your Armed Forces assessment, the number of questions and the duration you have for this section will depend on whether you are sitting the paper-based or computer-based version.

Subtest	Computer version	Paper version	Content
Word Knowledge (WK)	16 questions 8 minutes	35 questions 11 minutes	Correct word meaning

PLEASE NOTE: the Word Knowledge (WK) section **DOES** have an impact on your Armed Forces Qualification Test (AFQT) score. Be sure to improve your high school English ability.

The score for this subtest will be used along three other subtests to determine your AFQT score.

Use this chapter as a mini English lesson to recap on your general English knowledge. Below we have outlined the key areas that you should be focusing on:

WORD DEFINITIONS	WORD FAMILIES	VOCAB	PREFIXES
SUFFIXES	ADJECTIVES	NOUNS	VERBS
ADVERBS	PRONOUNS	ROOT WORDS	SYNONYMS
ANTONYMS	SIGNAL WORDS	CONTEXT	CONJUNCTION
PREPOSITIONS	TENSES	LONG / SHORT VOWELS	INTERJECTION

The Word Knowledge section of the ASVAB will consist of basic grammar, spelling and word knowledge. Brush up on these areas before attempting our practice questions.

Prefixes

PREFIXES: a letter or group of letters that you can add to the beginning of words in order to change their meanings.

Prefix	Example
A- or an-	Athesit, asexual, anarchronism
Ab-	Abnormal, abduct, abrupt
Abs-	Absorb, absent, abstract
Anti-	Antithesis, antiseptic, antisocial
Auto-	Autograph, automobile, autobiography
Bi-	Biannual, bicycle, biweekly
Circum-	Circumnavigate, circumcized
Com-	Commute, compassionate, compact
Con-	Contents, conform, contextual
Counter-	Counterexamples, counteract,
De-	Deduce, derange, detract
Deca-	Decade, decease, decoded
Extra-	Extraordinary, extracurricular
Fore-	Foreshadow, forecast, forebode
Geo-	Geographic, geology, geocentric
Hyper-	Hypertension, hyperactive, hyperbole
Il-	Illogical, illness, illiterate
Mal-	Maltreats, malnourished, maladapt
Multi-	Mulititude, multiplymulticultural
Ob-	Obstruct, obligation, obvious
Omni-	Omnivore, omnibus, omnipresence
Pre-	Preposition, preview, precaution
Que-	Query, question, quested
Re-	Restruct, revisit, rebuild
Semi-	Submarine, subway, subdued
Sub-	Subordinate,
Super-	Supervision, superior, superable
Tele-	Telephone, teleport, telescope
Trans-	Transport, transcribe, transform
Un-	Unhappy, unable, undeniable

Suffixes

SUFFIXES: letters that can be added to the end of a word in order to change its meaning.

Suffix	Example
-able	Agreeable, accountable, breakable
-age	Coverage, courage, breakage
-ance	Brilliance, appearance, performance
-ation	Hibernation, liberation, flirtation
-ed	Abandoned, adapted, encouraged
-en	Golden, strengthen, harden
-er	Attacker, keeper, bouncer
-ful	Bashful, delightful, forgetful
-ible	Accessible, destructible, reversible
-ic	Linguistic, agnoticic, anemic
-ical	Quizzical, metaphorical, hypothetical
-ing	Allowing, timing, building
-ion	Domination, allusion, detraction
-ise	Merchandise, globalise, criticise
-ish	Selfish, childish, bookish
-ism	Criticism, spiritualism, Darwinism
-ist	Socialist, anarchist, apologist
-ity	Abnormality, credibility, objectivity
-less	Hopeless, powerless, senseless
-let	Booklet, piglet, bracelet
-ly	Abruptly, amazingly, barely
-ment	Department, payment, commitment
-ness	Effectiveness, firmness, illness
-or	Tailor, honor, translator
-ous	Hazardous, wondrous, dangerous

Word Families

WORD FAMILIES: groups of words that have a common pattern or group of letters with the same sound.

Below we have listed lots of different examples of common word families.

-ACK	-AD	-AIL	-AIN
-AKE	-ALE	-ALL	-AM
-AME	-AN	-ANK	-AP
-AR	-ASH	-AT	-ATE
-AW	-AY	-EAT	-EEL
-EEP	-EET	-ELL	-EN
-ENT	-EST	-ICE	-ICK
-IDE	-IFE	-IGHT	-ILE
-ILL	-IN	-INE	ING
-INK	-IP	-IT	-OAT
-OCK	-OG	-OIL	-OKE
-OO	-OOD*	-OOF*	-OOK
-OOM	-OOL	-OON	-OOP
-OOT*	-ORE	-ORN	-OT
-OUGHT	-OULD	-OUSE	-OUT
-OP	-OW*	-OWN	-UCK
_UG	-UMP	-UN	-UNK

*Word families marked with an asterisk are because there are two different sounding ways.

For example, **'-OW'** can be read with a short vowel or a long vowel. The word **'COW'** and the word **'GROW'** both use the '-ow' word family, but sound very different.

Synonyms and Antonyms

Name	Meaning	Example
Synonym	A word that has the same or similar meaning to another word.	Synonyms of small = • Tiny • Little • Petite • Miniature
Antonym	A word that has the opposite meaning.	Antonyms of small = • Big • Fat • Large • Huge

Adjectives

ADJECTIVES are words that <u>describe nouns</u>.

Adjectives give sentences extra 'flavour' and detail, which allows for descriptive writing.

Remember, **NOUNS** are words that name something. Adjectives transform nouns by telling you more about how something looks or feels.

So, the adjective will describe that something in more detail.

The girl was **tiny**. ⇒	The adjective describes the _size_ of the girl.
The **black** cat. ⇒	The adjective describes the _colour_ of the cat.
I was **terrified**. ⇒	The adjective describes the _feelings_ of the noun – 'I'.

COMPARATIVE ADJECTIVES are used to compare qualities of two people or things.

SUPERLATIVE ADJECTIVES are used to compare qualities of a person or thing in relation to everyone in the group.

Adjective	Comparative	Superlative
One syllable = ending in E Strange, cute, late	Add 'r' Stranger, cuter, later	Add 'st' Strangest, cutest, latest
One syllable = ending in a vowel and consonant Big, slim, hot	Double consonant and add 'er' Bigger, slimmer, hotter	Double consonant and add 'est' Biggest, slimmest, hottest
One syllable = ending in more than one vowel or consonant Near, fast, light	Add 'er' Nearer, faster, lighter	Add 'est' Nearest, fastest, lightest
Two syllabled = ending in Y Happy, funny, lonely	Change Y to I and add 'er' Happier, funnier, lonelier	Change Y to I and add 'est' Happiest, funniest, loneliest
Two syllables or more = not ending in Y Beautiful, elegant	Use the word MORE More beautiful, more elegant	Use the word MOST Most beautiful, most elegant

Verbs and Adverbs

VERBS are 'doing' or 'being' or 'action' words.

These types of words are very useful because they tell us what someone is doing or what is happening.

<u>There are two types of verbs:</u>

1.   Doing words

2.   Being words

'DOING' VERBS describe an action.

She **plays** in the garden.

The boy **skates** once a week.

The child **kicks** the football.

Harry **eats** his roast dinner.

'BEING' VERBS are other types of verbs that tell you how something is.

These type of verbs come from the verb 'to be'.

I **am** healthy.

We **are** going on holiday.

We **were** late for class.

It **was** going to be a great day.

ADVERBS describe verbs.

Adverbs are used to tell you when or how an action was done.

Most adverbs end in 'ly' – quickly, silently, dramatically etc.

However, not all adverbs follow this rule – late .

Adverbs also describe adjectives:

• Quite, nearly, really and very are all adverbs.

They provide extra information about the adjective – "quite big" or "really annoying".

Nouns and Pronouns

NOUNS are names of things.

Below are four types of nouns:

1. PROPER NOUNS
2. COMMON NOUNS

3. COLLECTIVE NOUNS

4. ABSTRACT NOUNS

PROPER NOUNS are the names of people or places or objects or days/months of the year.

Germany	Bedgebury Avenue	River Thames
(place)	(place)	(place)
Uppersfield United	Friday	April
(teams)	(day)	(month)
Elizabeth	Ryan	Harrison
(people)	(people)	(people)

A key thing to remember is that proper nouns will **ALWAYS** have a capital letter.

COMMON NOUNS are words we use every day. They are general, non-specific words for people, places or objects or things.

gardens	mountains	house
(place)	(place)	(place)
baby	woman	man
(people)	(people)	(people)
fork	chair	penguin
(object)	(object)	(animals)

COLLECTIVE NOUNS are nouns that describe groups of things.

team	crowd	pack
(team of players)	(crowd of people)	(pack of wolves)
swarm	flock	herd
(swarm of bees)	(flock of birds)	(herd of sheep)

ABSTRACT NOUNS are words that describe things that you cannot see, touch, taste, smell or hear.

These words could describe particular emotions that someone might be feeling, and they could also describe ideas.

happiness	jealousy	anger
freedom	bravery	wisdom
love	hate	fear
curiosity	self-esteem	childhood

PRONOUNS are used to replace nouns.

Pronouns help you to avoid repeating the same word over and over and over again.

1st person

I	Me	We	Us

2nd person

You

3rd person

He / him	She / her	They / them	It

Relative pronouns

Who	That	Which	Where / When

Possessive pronouns

Mine / Yours	Ours / Theirs	His / Hers	Its

Conjunctions

CONJUNCTIONS are very basic and easy to understand!

They are short words or phrases that are used to join words together, in order to make a sentence.

Conjunctions can also be used to link sentences together, in order to make them flow better. This means you don't have to keep putting a full stop and ending the sentence abruptly.

- That sentence might read better joined by the following sentence, with the use of a conjunction.

THINK of CONJUNCTIONS like a JIGSAW PUZZLE.

TYPES OF CONJUNCTIONS

Below is a list of some of the common types of conjunctions that you will need to know.

AND	SO	BUT	YET
BECAUSE	UNTIL	HOWEVER	SINCE
EVEN THOUGH	SUDDENLY	AS	ALTHOUGH
ALTERNATIVELY	MEANWHILE	AT LAST	PERHAPS
NEVERTHELESS	DESPITE	WHENEVER	FURTHERMORE
THEREFORE	WHILE	BESIDES	FINALLY
IN ADDITION TO	NEXT	EXCEPT	SIMILARLY
IN FACT	ALSO	INDEED	EVEN SO

When it comes to writing any piece of text, it is important that you are able to use the correct verb form, to indicate whether something is happening, has happened, or will happen.

This is known as using the correct **VERB TENSE**.

There are three tenses that you need to be aware of:

PAST

- The past tense indicates something that has already happened, or used to happen.

- It can be used to describe something that has just happened.

PRESENT

- The present tense indicates something happening at this very moment.

- It can also be used to describe something that happens regularly.

FUTURE

- The future tense indicates something that is going to happen in the future.

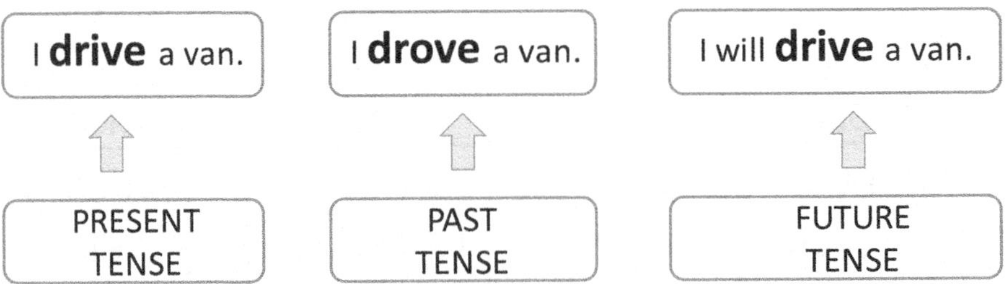

WORD KNOWLEDGE QUICK TIPS

- Ensure that your vocabulary is at its strongest. You need to make sure that you have a good understanding of different words and their meaning.

- Make sure you spend time practising your grammar and spelling.

- Identify words with similar meanings. You will need to be able to differentiate between these.

- Focus on key areas such as word adjectives, nouns, verbs, conjunctions, tenses, synonyms, antonyms, prepositions etc.

- If you don't know the answer, take an educated guess. You can eliminate some of the options you know to be incorrect.

- Keep an eye on the time. Remember you only have 11 minutes to answer all 35 questions for the paper-version of the ASVAB (8 minutes to answer 16 questions on the computer-version). That works out to be around 20 seconds per question!

- As with any test, it is important to undergo in-depth revision. The only way to enhance your knowledge is to revise your basic English skills. Break up your revision time using a timetable. Focus on the areas that you are not so confident with.

WORD KNOWLEDGE *PRACTICE QUESTIONS*

For each question, work out what the word underlined means. For sentences with words underlined, you need to find the most SIMILAR meaning.

QUESTION 1

Internecine most nearly means...

A. Advanced.

B. Encouraging.

C. Destructive.

D. Alienation.

QUESTION 2

Nugatory most nearly means...

A. Tribulation.

B. Enthusiastic.

C. Favourable.

D. Worthless.

QUESTION 3

It was a mistake to <u>disparge</u> their achievements.

A. Blame.

B. Honor.

C. Forget.

D. Underestimate.

QUESTION 4

It was a <u>deceitful</u> act.

A. Powerful.

B. Treacherous.

C. Noble.

D. Worthy.

QUESTION 5

<u>Dispensation</u> most nearly means...

A. Succulent.

B. Triumphant.

C. Recompense.

D. Exemption.

QUESTION 6

It was an <u>anfractuous</u> path.

A. Outstanding.

B. Circuitous.

C. Unknown.

D. Meandrous.

QUESTION 7

<u>Fuscous</u> most nearly means...

A. Dark and sombre in color.

B. Thick and sticky consistency.

C. Imaginary or fabricated.

D. Wasted material.

QUESTION 8

They had the intellect to <u>previse</u> the outcome.

A. Create and perform spontaneously.

B. Causing harm.

C. Forese.

D. To cease.

QUESTION 9

<u>Reminiscence</u> most nearly means...

A. Beacon.

B. Recollection.

C. Hallucination.

D. Tedious.

QUESTION 10

The word most opposite in meaning to <u>fluctuate</u> is...

A. Insignificant.

B. Retribution.

C. Zealous.

D. Steady.

ANSWERS TO WORD KNOWLEDGE PRACTICE QUESTIONS

Q1. C. Destructive.

Q2. D. Worthless.

Q3. D. Underestimate.

Q4. B. Treacherous.

Q5. D. Exemption.

Q6. B. Circuitous.

Q7. A. Dark and sombre in color.

Q8. C. Foresee the future.

Q9. B. Recollection.

Q10. D. Steady.

Now move on to the Paragraph Comprehension subtest of the ASVAB.

PARAGRAPH COMPREHENSION

The Paragraph Comprehension section of the ASVAB requires you to read a paragraph and understand what you have just read.

During this section of your Armed Forces assessment, the number of questions and the duration you have will depend on whether you are sitting the paper-based or computer-based version.

Subtest	Computer version	Paper version	Content
Paragraph Comprehension (PC)	11 questions 22 minutes	15 questions 13 minutes	Read a passage and answer questions

PLEASE NOTE: the Paragraph Comprehension (PC) section **DOES** have an impact on your Armed Forces Qualification Test (AFQT) score. Be sure to improve your high school English ability in order to ensure higher ASVAB marks.

The score for this subtest will be used alongside three other subtests to determine your AFQT score.

Use this chapter as a mini English lesson to recap on your general English knowledge. Below we have outlined the key areas that you should be focusing on:

MAIN IDEAS/ ARGUMENTS	SPECIFIC DETAILS	DRAWING CONCLUSIONS	PARAPHRASING
INTERPRET	WORD MEANING	IMPLICATIONS	RELATIONSHIP BETWEEN IDEAS

The Word Knowledge section of the ASVAB will consist of basic grammar, spelling and word knowledge. Brush up on these areas before attempting our practice questions.

Our advice is to practice questions relating to Word Knowledge (WK). This will allow you to answer questions in this section that refer to word meaning and context.

Working Out the Main Idea or Argument

When you read a piece of text, you should be able to recognize the main idea or underlying argument. Sometimes, the main idea will be directly stated, and sometimes it will only be implied.

Your task will be to analyse the information presented to you, and work out the overall aim/idea of the text.

If you are unsure about what the main argument is, re-read the passage and highlight key points.

Consider the following points:

- *What is the writer saying?*

- *What is the purpose of the passage?*

Asking yourself the above questions will allow you to pinpoint key features of the passage. Generally, reading the first and last lines of the passage will give you some indication as to what the main ideas of the passage are.

Keep Track of Details

With regards to details, you need to ensure that you are able to detect the key details from a piece of information, and disregard any irrelevant information.

Our best advice is to use a highlighter pen, and highlight key information as you read through the text.

Of course, you're now probably wondering how you determine what is key and what is not.

Look out for key things which would answer the following:

- *Who?*

- *What?*

- *When?*

- *Where?*

- *Why?*

Understand Different Word Meanings

When reading comprehension, you need to pay attention to the wording used. Sometimes, a word in a sentence is used in the most common manner, whilst other times it can be used in a less well-known manner.

You will need to read the passage carefully, and make sure you know why certain words are used, and work out what words mean.

For example, writing over different centuries varies considerably. A word used in the 18th century can have a very different meaning to how it is used today.

- For example, the word 'clue' or (clew) was often used to describe a ball of yarn. Now the word is used to provide hints and give insight into something, in order to work something out.

- An example is the word 'spinster'. Spinsters used to be a woman who spun. Now it is used to describe a woman who is unmarried.

Analyzing the Text

With regards to analyzing, it is important that you are doing more than simply picking out key facts and information. If you are asked to analyze a passage, you need to be able to draw conclusions and make assumptions and inferences based on what you have read.

Consider the following points when analyzing a text:

- *Offer a balanced overview of the text.*

- *Remain objective and impersonal.*

- *Draw a fair conclusion.*

- *Investigate and analyze the main issues of the text.*

PARAGRAPH COMPREHENSION

QUICK TIPS

- Read each paragraph quickly and pinpoint the key details.

- Read the paragraph closely to analyze the text in more detail.

- Read the question carefully. Look out for sneaky words such as "except", "not", "always", "never" etc. These words change what is actually being asked.

- Some questions will require you to fact check. Other questions will require you to summarize what you have read. Some questions will require you to infer and then come to a conclusion.

- If you don't know the answer, take an educated guess. You can eliminate some of the options you know to be incorrect.

- Keep an eye on the time. Remember you only have 13 minutes to answer all 15 questions for the paper-version of the ASVAB (20 minutes to answer 11 questions on the computer-version). That works out to be around 50 seconds per question!

- As with any test, it is important to undergo in-depth revision. The only way to enhance your knowledge is to revise your basic comprehensive skills. Break up your revision time using a timetable. Focus on the areas that you are not so confident with.

PARAGRAPH COMPREHENSION

> A fire has occurred in a nightclub belonging to Harry James. One person died in the fire, which occurred at 11pm on Saturday night. The club was insured for less than its value.

QUESTION 1

The fire was caused by...

A. Arson.

B. Electrical fault.

C. Faulty wiring.

D. None of the above.

> At 1800 hours today police issued a statement in relation to the crime scene in Armstrong Road. Police have been examining the scene all day and reports suggest that it may be murder. Forensic officers have been visiting the incident and inform us that the whole street has been cordoned off and nobody will be allowed through. Police say that the street involved will be closed for another 18 hours and no access will be available to anyone during this time.

QUESTION 2

What time would the street be open to the public?

A. It's already open.

B. 8pm that evening.

C. 12 noon the following day.

D. None of the above.

QUESTION 3

The word 'cordoned', as used in this passage mostly means...

A. Inaccessible.

B. Permit required.

C. Opened.

D. None of the above.

"It's gone. The ring has gone!" Freddie looked up from peering through one of the glass cabinets, hoping to find the perfect item of jewellery for his best friend, Scarlett. He was in a small jewellery shop in the city centre of CapeTown. The walls were painted in a dark red, with pictures hung crookedly all around. The floor was tiled and scuffed. The harsh lighting made it difficult to see what you were looking at, but somehow it made it feel cosier, more inviting.

Freddie stood in the farthest corner from the tills, but the sound of the trembling young girl grabbed his attention.

QUESTION 4

What would be a good title for the passage?

A. Thiefs in the Night.

B. My Account of Thieves.

C. Freddie and the Supermarket Store.

D. Freddie and the Stolen Ring.

Every child needs to understand the importance of road safety. Here is an outline of road safety. Remember, this can save a life!

Try and use zebra, puffin, pelican or toucan crossings where possible. Does the road have a footbridge you can go over? Does the road have islands which you can wait on? Is the road controlled by school crossing patrol?

If none of these are available to you, find a place where you can see every direction. Make sure you are visible by standing in a place where you're not hidden. Even wearing bright or florescent clothing will help you to be seen.

Don't stand behind parked cars, or on corners. This is not a safe place to cross.

Don't stand too close to the kerb when looking to see whether or not it is safe to cross. A vehicle or cyclist might be driving too close to the kerb and this will likely cause an accident.

QUESTION 5

According to the passage, what is the first step in road safety?

A. Look and listen!

B. Don't rush – if traffic is coming, wait!

C. Find a safe place to cross.

D. Make sure you are a good distance away from the kerb.

QUESTION 6

From reading the passage, you can assume that the text is meant to...

A. Persuade.

B. Explain.

C. Instruct.

D. Argue.

Global warming is already having an impact on our community, and without taking action, the issue will continue to become more of a concern and will affect the future of our world.

It doesn't just mean that the weather will get somewhat warmer; this is not always the case. As the planet begins to heat, climate patterns will fluctuate and will result in extreme and unpredictable weather conditions. This means that across the world, some weather conditions may be extremely hot, whilst others will experience torrential rain or plummeting temperatures. These are a direct consequence of the way in which the planet has been treated.

QUESTION 7

In the second paragraph, the author uses the term "fluctuate". Based on the context of the passage, what do you think this mostly means?

A. Planet welfare.

B. Weather dependant.

C. Persistent.

D. Goes up and down.

QUESTION 8

According to the passage, we can mostly assume that...

A. Deforestation plays no role in global warming.

B. Burning fossil fuels is a contributing factor to global warming.

C. Global warming is unstoppable.

D. Global warming is a result of man.

The skeleton works by the bones being supported by joints. Joints are where two bones join together. These joints allows us to bend. Kneecaps, ankles and wrists are all examples of bone joints.

Muscles are attached to our bones with tendons. They work in pairs and stretch out, which allows us to be mobile. When one of the muscles contracts, the other relaxes. The heart is the most important muscle in the body.

QUESTION 9

The word 'contracts', as used in the passage, most nearly means...

A. Weakens.

B. Grow.

C. Fixated.

D. Movement.

Strand by strand, Webster created an articulate infrastructure; a structure so defined and carefully constructed, that it made all others seem unrefined. Clear light lines that, although appeared fragile and breakable, were actually a strong, valuable asset to the world in which he lived.

"It's all in the spinning," Webster smiled as he continued to finish off his masterpiece. There was nothing Webster liked doing more than spending time with his companion, Toby. Together they would create a sense of security and triumph – Webster's definition of perfection.

QUESTION 10

The word 'infrastructure', as used in the passage, can be most associated with...

A. A path.

B. A tunnel.

C. A hair.

D. A web.

ANSWERS TO PARAGRAPH COMPREHENSION PRACTICE QUESTIONS

Q1. D. None of the above.

Q2. C. 12 noon the following day.

Q3. A. Inaccessible.

Q4. D. Freddie and the Stolen Ring.

Q5. C. Find a safe place to cross.

Q6. C. Instruct.

Q7. D. Goes up and down.

Q8. D. Global warming is a result of man.

Q9. D. Movement.

Q10. D. A web.

Now move on to the Mathematics Knowledge subtest of the ASVAB.

MATHEMATICS KNOWLEDGE

The Mathematics Knowledge section of the ASVAB requires you to have a basic high school level of mathematical concepts.

During this section of your Armed Forces assessment, the number of questions and the duration you have for this section will depend on whether you are sitting the paper-based or computer-based version.

Subtest	Computer version	Paper version	Content
Mathematics Knowledge (MK)	16 questions 20 minutes	25 questions 24 minutes	High school mathematical knowledge

PLEASE NOTE: the Mathematics Knowledge (MK) section **DOES** have an impact on your Armed Forces Qualification Test (AFQT) score. Be sure to improve your high school English ability.

The score for this subtest will be used along three other subtests to determine your AFQT score.

Use this chapter as a mini Maths lesson to recap on your general Maths knowledge. Below we have outlined the key areas that you should be focusing on:

INTEGERS	PRIME NUMBERS	FACTORS	COMPOSITE NUMBERS
SQUARE ROOTS	RECIPROCAL	ROUNDING	ORDER OF OPERATIONS
PATTERNS AND SEQENCES	FRACTIONS	DECIMALS	PERCENTS
SCALE DRAWINGS	RATES	INTEREST	ALGEBRA
ANGLES	INEQUALITIES	TRIANGLES	CIRCLES
VOLUME	AREA	PERIMETER	SOLVING PROBLEMS

The Mathematics Knowledge section of the ASVAB will consist of basic mathematical knowledge. Brush up on these areas before attempting our practice questions.

Mathematical Terminology

Just like in the literary sections of the ASVAB, the mathematical tests also require you to learn some mathematical terminology.

See **APPENDIX B** for a list of terminology that you should familiarize yourself with before attempting the test of this chapter.

Order of Operations

BIDMAS is an acrostic which can be used to remember how you should go about solving maths questions.

BIDMAS is a great way to remember which order you should work out operations in a calculation that has more than one operation.

The order of operations is as follows:

Brackets ( )

Indices X^2

Division ÷

Multiplication X

Addition +

Subtraction -

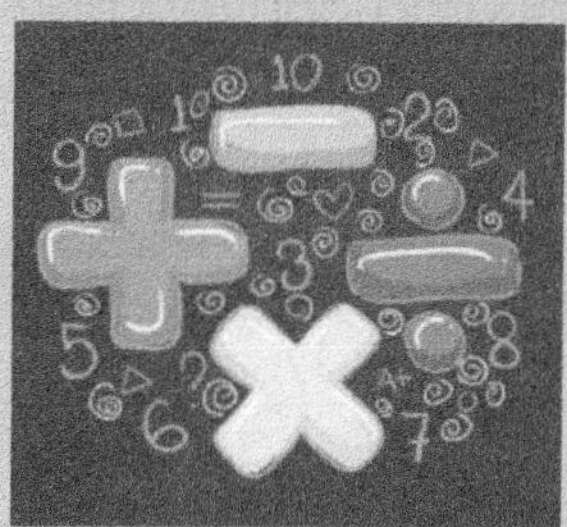

Integers

Integers are whole numbers – whether they're positive or negative. The ASVAB assessment will often require you to work with different integers.

Inequalities

INEQUALITY SYMBOLS

>	Greater than.
<	Less than.
≥	Greater than or equal to.
≤	Less than or equal to.

<u>For example:</u>

- 5,000 > 2,000 = 5,000 is GREATER THAN 2,000.

- 300 < 600 = 300 is LESS THAN 600.

Fractions, Decimals, and Percentages

Fractions, decimals and percentages are all ways of describing **PART** of a whole number.

You can convert between fractions, decimals and percentages, and you need to learn how to do this!

FRACTION	DECIMAL	PERCENTAGE
$^1/_2$	0.5	50%
$^1/_4$	0.25	25%
$^3/_4$	0.75	75%
$^1/_3$	0.3333…	33 $^1/_3$%
$^2/_3$	0.6666…	66 $^2/_3$%
$^1/_5$	0.2	20%
$^2/_5$	0.4	40%
$^1/_{10}$	0.1	10%
$^2/_{10}$	0.2	20%

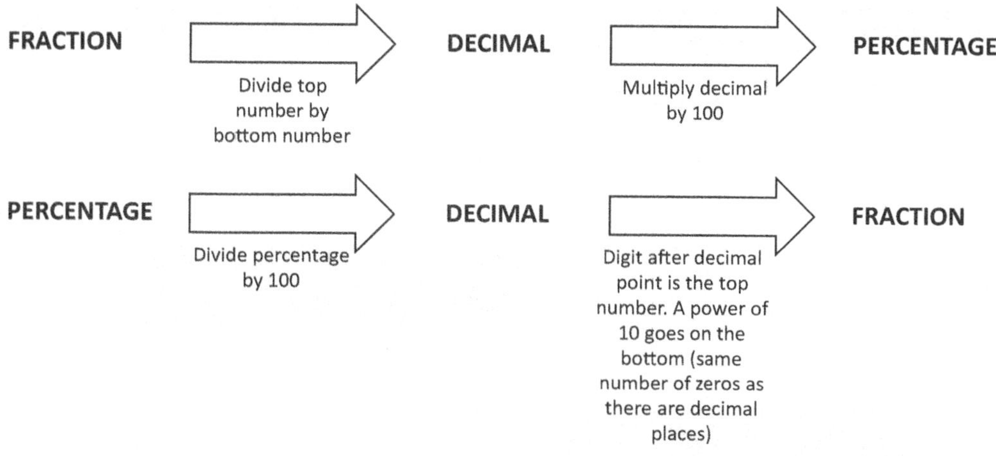

Fractions

$\frac{2}{5}$

→ The top number is called the **NUMERATOR**.

→ The bottom number is called the **DENOMINATOR**.

THE NUMERATOR

The numerator number tells you how many 'bits' we are <u>trying to work out</u>.

THE DENOMINATOR

The denominator number tells you how many bits there are '<u>altogether</u>'.

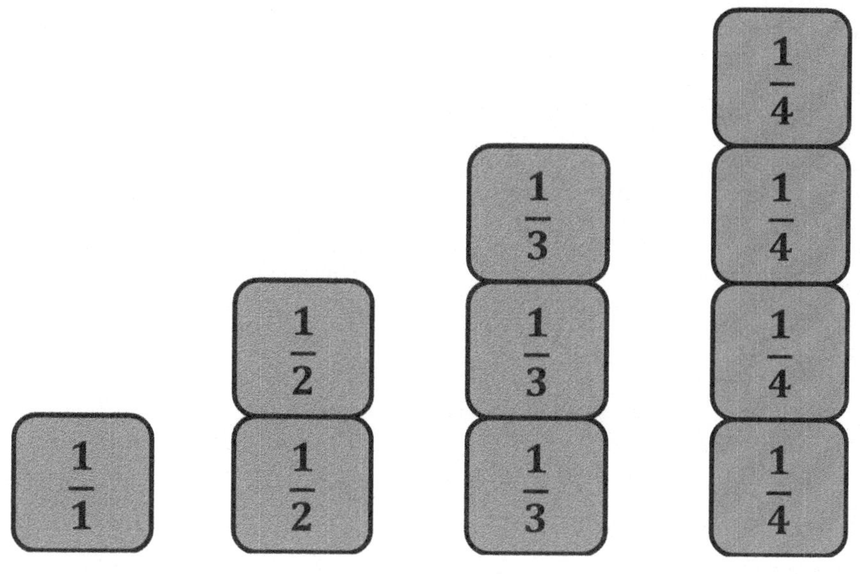

Equivalent Fractions

Equivalent = 'the same as'.

Equivalent fractions look different, but are actually representing the same thing.

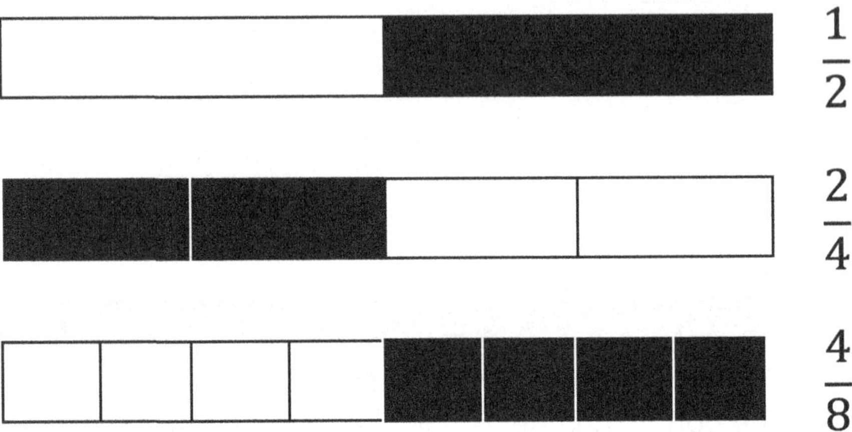

Simplifying Fractions

The word **SIMPLIFYING** simply means 'to make it simple'. Sometimes, you can simplify fractions in order to make them easier to understand.

This is similar to finding equivalent fractions. However, instead of multiplying, you will divide – you want to make the fraction smaller!

Mixed Fractions

MIXED FRACTIONS have both an integer and a fraction.

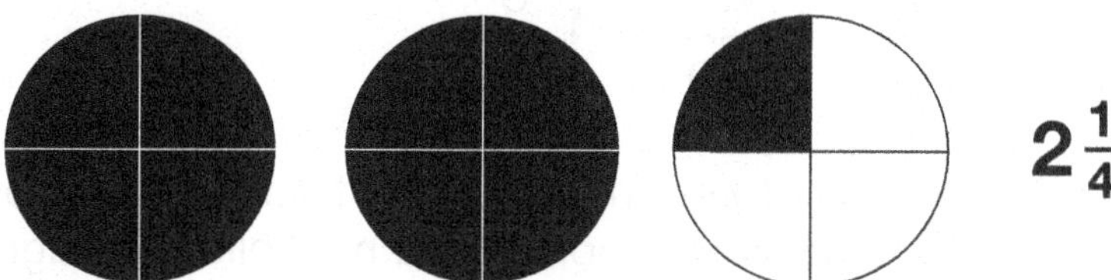

$$2\frac{1}{4}$$

An IMPROPER FRACTION is where the top number of the fraction is bigger than the bottom number of the fraction.

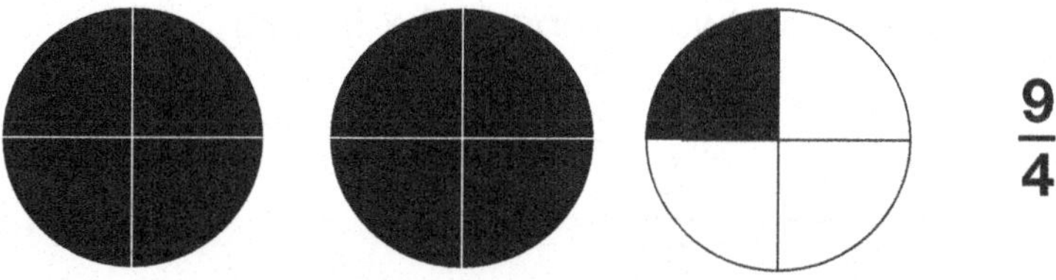

$$\frac{9}{4}$$

To write a mixed fraction as an improper fraction:	To write an improper fraction as a mixed fraction:
$4\frac{2}{3}$	$\dfrac{16}{5}$
• Multiply the whole number by the bottom number of the fraction (12). Add the top number of the fraction (12 + 2 = 14). • This number will form the top part of the fraction. • Leave the bottom number of the fraction as it is: $\dfrac{14}{3}$	• How many 5s go into 16 exactly? Answer = 3 • How many is left over? Answer = 1 • So, 3 is the whole number. • 1 is the top part of the fraction, and the bottom number will be the same: $3\frac{1}{5}$

Adding and Subtracting Fractions

CROSSBOW METHOD

$$\frac{3}{4} + \frac{2}{5} = \frac{15+8}{20} = \frac{23}{20} = 1\frac{3}{20}$$

Draw two diagonal lines through both of the fractions as shown. (This forms the **CROSS** which looks like a multiplication sign).

It tells you to multiply the 3 by 5 = 15
It tells you to multiply the 4 by 2 = 8.

Then draw your **BOW** (from the bottom number of the first fraction to the bottom number of the second fraction).

Again, multiply these two numbers: 4 x 5 = 20

$$\frac{4}{7} - \frac{1}{3} = \frac{12-7}{21} = \frac{5}{21}$$

Draw two diagonal lines through both of the fractions as shown. (This forms the **CROSS** which looks like a multiplication sign).

It tells you to multiply the 4 by 3 = 12
It tells you to multiply the 7 by 1 = 7.
12 - 7 = 5

Then draw your **BOW** (from the bottom number of the first fraction to the bottom number of the second fraction).

Again, multiply these two numbers: 7 x 3 = 21

Multiplying and Dividing Fractions

ARROW METHOD

$$\frac{5}{9} \times \frac{3}{5} = \frac{15}{45} = \frac{3}{9} = \frac{1}{3}$$

Draw an arrow through the two top numbers and multiply.
5 x 3 = 15

Draw an arrow through the two bottom numbers.
9 x 5 = 45

Done! (Some fractions will be able to be simplified, as shown in the above example).

$$\frac{4}{7} \div \frac{3}{4} = \frac{4}{7} \times \frac{4}{3} = \frac{16}{21}$$

This is actually quite simple. Turn the second fraction upside down. Change the divide sum to a multiply, and then use the **SAME** method as if you were multiplying.

You will get the answer correct every time!

<u>Key thing to remember</u>:

When you are dividing two fractions, don't forget to turn the second fraction **UPSIDE DOWN** before you multiply the numbers.

Work Out a Fraction of a Number

<u>To find a fraction of something:</u>

1) Divide the whole number by the bottom number of the fraction.

2) Then, multiply by the top number of the fraction.

<u>Alternatively:</u>

1) Multiply the whole number by the top number of the fraction.

2) Then, divide the number by the bottom number of the fraction.

EXAMPLE

Work out $\dfrac{5}{8}$ of \$272.

STEP 1

Divide 272 by the bottom number of the fraction (8).

- $272 \div 8 = 34$

STEP 2

Multiply 34 by the top number of the fraction (5).

- $34 \times 5 = \$170.$

So, $\dfrac{5}{8}$ of \$272 is \$170.

Decimals

Like fractions, decimals are another way of writing a number that is not whole.

A decimal is in fact 'in-between numbers'.

6.48 ⟶ This is in between the number 6 and the number 7.

USING PLACE VALUES

In order to work out what the decimal is representing, you should use place values.

These include: units, tenths, hundredths and thousandths.

Adding and Subtracting Decimals

0.5 + 0.62

How to work it out:

$$\begin{array}{r} 0.5 \\ +\ 0.62 \\ \hline 1.12 \end{array}$$

The decimal points need to be lined up!

Your answer should begin by adding the decimal point in first, and then add up the columns from right to left.

2.46 - 1.35

How to work it out:

```
  2.46
- 1.35
  ----
  1.11
```

The decimal points need to be lined up!

Your answer should begin by adding the decimal point in first, and then subtracting the columns from right to left.

Multiplying and Dividing Decimals

2.5 x 0.2

How to work it out:

- Remove the decimal points.

    25 x 2 = 50

- Now add in the decimal points. **REMEMBER**, you need to work out how many numbers come **AFTER** the decimal point in the question.

- You should notice that two numbers come after the decimal point (the .5 and the .2).

- Therefore 2 numbers need to come after the decimal point in the answer.

    25 x 2 = 50

- So the answer would be 0.50 or 0.5. It is usually written 0.5 (the 0 at the end is not necessary.

REMEMBER: division is easy if you are dividing by whole numbers. You need to move the decimal points in both numbers the same number of places.

$5.39 \div 1.1$

<u>How to work it out:</u>

Move the decimal point 1 space.

$53.9 \div 11.$

- Now ignore the decimal point in 53.9, do long division and then add it in at the end.

```
        049
    11 | 539
       - 0
        ___
         0
        ___
        53
      - 44
        ___
        99
      - 99
        ___
         0
```

Put the decimal point in the answer directly above the decimal point in the question.

$$\text{ANSWER} = 11 \overline{)\,53.9\,}^{\,04.9}$$

Recurring Decimals

A recurring decimal is a decimal that goes on forever. For example, $0.\dot{4}$ means 0.444444.....

If two dots are used, this shows the beginning and the end of the recurring numbers. For example $0.\dot{6}1\dot{3}$ means 0.613613613...

Percentages

Percentages are used to work out part of a number. For example 25% of something is equivalent to $\frac{1}{4}$ or 0.25

Percent ⟶ out of 100

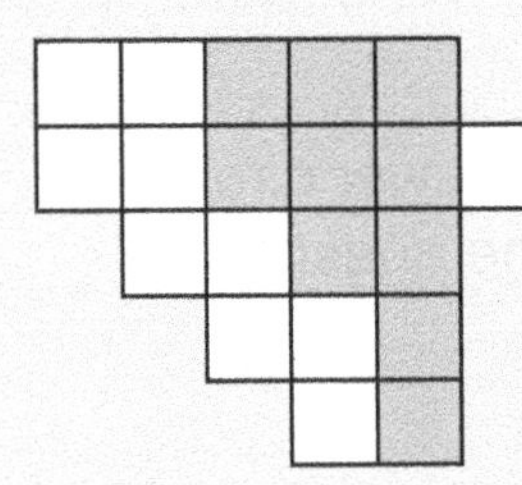

- To work out what percentage of this shape is shaded, you first need to work out the total number of squares.

Total number of squares = 20.

- Now work out the number of squares shaded.

Number of squares shaded = 10.

- There are 20 equal parts which means each square represents 5% (5 x 20 = 100). So, 5% x 10 (shaded squares) = 50%

Find x% of y

To work out the percentage of a number, i.e. 35% of 300, you should **ALWAYS** use the following method, as it guarantees that you get the correct answer.

35% of 300

Step 1 = 300 ÷ 100 = 3

Step 2 = 3 x 35 = 105.

Step 3 = 105 is 35% of 300.

Alternatively, you can convert the percentage into a decimal. So 35% become 0.35 x 300 = 105.

Expressing X as a Percentage of Y

To express a number as a percentage of something else, you will need to divide x by y and then multiply by 100.

Write 30 cents as a percentage of $1.20

Step 1

Convert the dollars into cents. You need to work with the same units.

Step 2

Divide 30 cents by 120 cents.

$30 \div 120 = 0.25$

Step 3

Multiply this by 100.

$0.25 \times 100 = 25\%$

Rounding Up and Rounding Down

When the units are LESS THAN 5, you will round down.

When the units are MORE THAN 5, you will round up.

If the unit IS 5, you will also round up!

There are different ways you could be asked to round a number up or down. This is usually asked by using the words 'to the nearest'.

Sometimes, you will be asked to round a number to a significant figure. This is very similar to rounding to decimal places, except that you will focus on the number.

<u>How to round a number to significant figures:</u>

STEP 1

Identify the number of significant figures you are working with. For example, if you are trying to work out 2 s.f. then you will focus on the **SECOND** digit.

STEP 2

Then, look at the next digit to the right of this number. This is called the **DECIDER**.

- If it's 5 or higher, you will round up.
- If it's 4 or less, you will leave the number as it is.

STEP 3

Once you have rounded the number, you should fill up the gaps to complete the number (zeroes will be needed up to the decimal point).

Multiples

Factors are numbers that can be divided **EXACTLY** into other numbers.

Work out the factors of 60.

1 x 60 = 60	4 x 15 = 60
2 x 30 = 60	5 x 12 = 60
3 x 20 = 60	6 x 10 = 60

Multiples

<u>How to find the least common multiple (lcm):</u>

Finding the 'common' multiples of numbers means finding a number that they both have in common.

EXAMPLE

Find the lowest common multiple of 2 and 5.

Step 1

Write out the first few multiples of 2.

2, 4, 6, 8, 10…

Step 2

Write out the first few multiples of 5.

5, 10, 15, 20, 25…

Step 3

Find the lowest multiple that both 2 and 5 have in common.

Step 4

The lowest common multiple for 2 and 5 is 10. (There is no smaller number that is a multiple of 2 and 5, therefore this is the correct answer).

Prime Numbers

Prime numbers are numbers that cannot be divided by anything else apart from the number 1 and itself.
All prime numbers up to 100 have been shaded.

1	2	3	4	5	6	7	8	9	10
11	12	13	14	15	16	17	18	19	20
21	22	23	24	25	26	27	28	29	30
31	32	33	34	35	36	37	38	39	40
41	42	43	44	45	46	47	48	49	50
51	52	53	54	55	56	57	58	59	60
61	62	63	64	65	66	67	68	69	70
71	72	73	74	75	76	77	78	79	80
81	82	83	84	85	86	87	88	89	90
91	92	93	94	95	96	97	98	99	100

Percentage Increase and Percentage Decrease

To work out the percentage increase of a set of data, you need to remember this formula:

PERCENT INCREASE % = DIFFERENCE ÷ ORIGINAL NUMBER X 100

To work out the percentage decrease of a set of data, you need to remember this formula:

PERCENT DECREASE % = DIFFERENCE ÷ ORIGINAL NUMBER X 100

Ratios

Ratios are a way of showing how things are shared.

The process of simplifying is quite easy. All you have to do is find a number that both values of the ratio can be divided by.

The ratio will be in its simplest form, when there are no numbers that can be divided into both values of the ratio.

EXAMPLE

Simplify 40 : 60. Write your answer in its simplest form.

Step 1

Both '40' and '60' can be divided by 10.

- If you divide both numbers by 10, you get the ratio: 4 : 6

Step 2

Both '4' and '6' can be divided by 2.

- If you divide both numbers by 2, you would get the ratio: 2 : 3

Step 3

No other numbers can be divided equally into 2 and 3, so 2 : 3 is the simplest form of 40 : 60.

See how the ratios 40 : 60, 4 : 6 and 2 : 3 are all equivalent ratios = they all mean the same thing!

Proportion

Proportional division is very simple to understand.

This is where you will be given a total, and you have to divide that total by the two parts of the ratio.

There are 3 steps that you need to follow in order to work out proportional division correctly.

STEP 1

Add up the two parts of the ratio.

STEP 2

Divide the total by the number of both parts (the number you get after adding both parts of the ratio).

STEP 3

Multiply that number by the number of parts you are trying to work out.

Angles

An angle is a way of measuring a turn. The size of the angle will determine the ANGLE NAME.

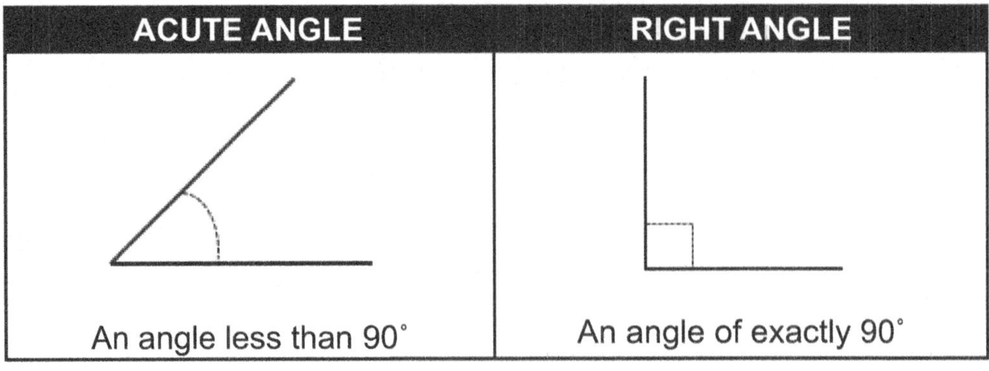

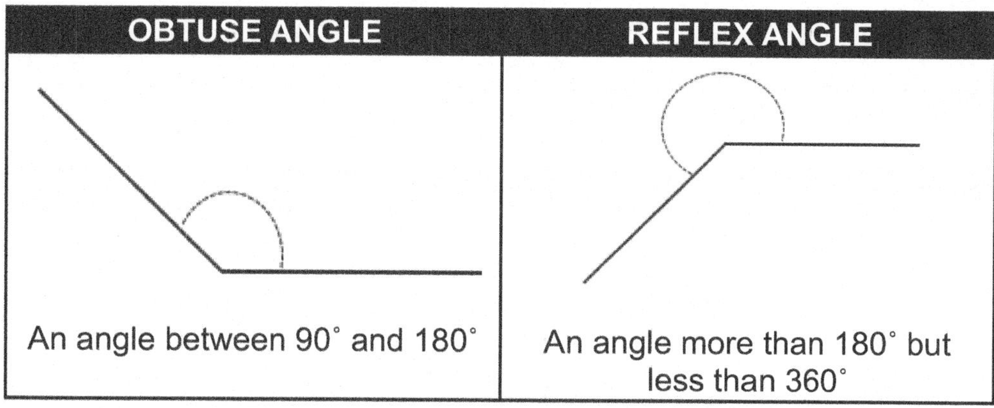

These names are often used to describe triangles.

Angles in a Triangle

The angles in a triangle will **ALWAYS** add up to 180°.

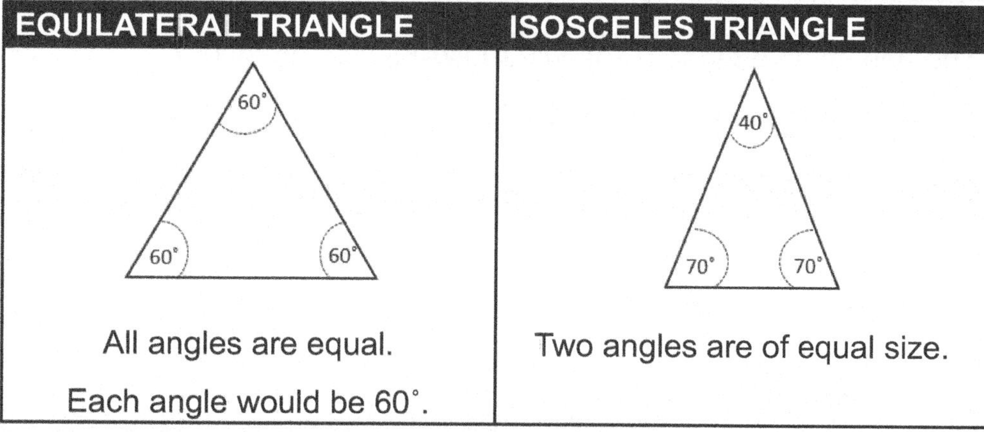

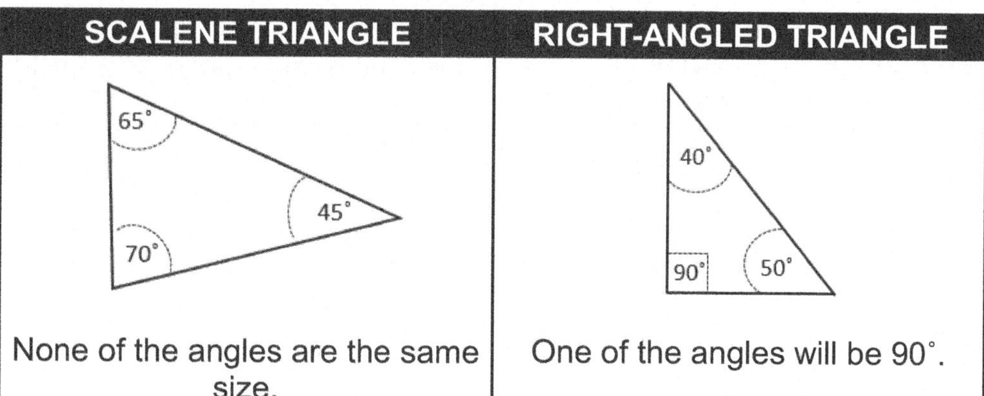

Angles in a Quadrilateral

The angles in a quadrilateral will **ALWAYS** add up to 360°.

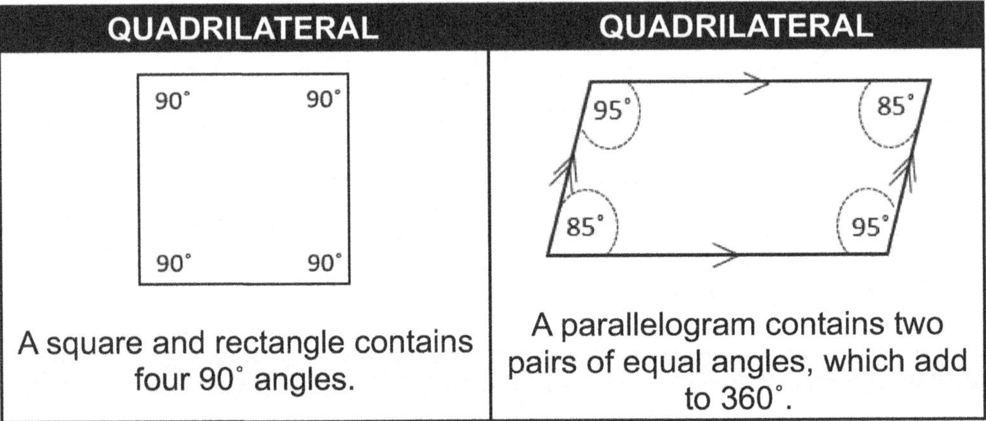

A square and rectangle contains four 90° angles.

A parallelogram contains two pairs of equal angles, which add to 360°.

ANGLES OF STRAIGHT LINES AND CIRCLES

The angles on a straight line will **ALWAYS** add up to 180°.

The angles in a circle will **ALWAYS** add up to 360°.

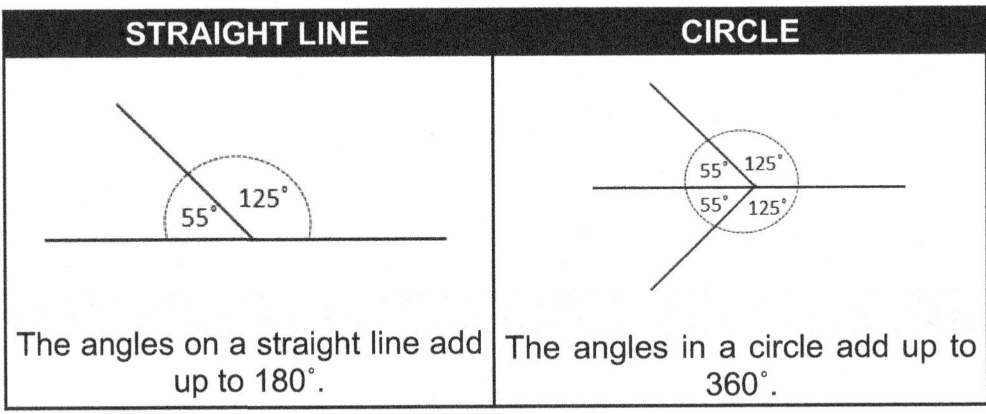

The angles on a straight line add up to 180°.

The angles in a circle add up to 360°.

2D and 3D Shapes

2D shapes are shapes that only have two dimensions – length and width.

When it comes to 2D shapes, there are two types:

- Regular polygons;
- Irregular polygons.

Regular Polygons

TRIANGLE	NO. OF SIDES	LINES OF SYMMETRY	ROTATIONAL SYMMETRY
	• 3 sides	• 3 lines of symmetry	• Rotational symmetry of order 3

QUADRILATERAL	NO. OF SIDES	LINES OF SYMMETRY	ROTATIONAL SYMMETRY
	• 4 sides	• 4 lines of symmetry	• Rotational symmetry of order 4

PENTAGON	NO. OF SIDES	LINES OF SYMMETRY	ROTATIONAL SYMMETRY
	• 5 sides	• 5 lines of symmetry	• Rotational symmetry of order 5

HEXAGON	NO. OF SIDES	LINES OF SYMMETRY	ROTATIONAL SYMMETRY
	• 6 sides	• 6 lines of symmetry	• Rotational symmetry of order 6

HEPTAGON	NO. OF SIDES	LINES OF SYMMETRY	ROTATIONAL SYMMETRY
	• 7 sides	• 7 lines of symmetry	• Rotational symmetry of order 7

OCTAGON	NO. OF SIDES	LINES OF SYMMETRY	ROTATIONAL SYMMETRY
	• 8 sides	• 8 lines of symmetry	• Rotational symmetry of order 8

Irregular Polygons

An irregular polygon is a shape which has different size lengths. All of its interior angles are of different size.

Let's go through some of the properties of some irregular polygon shapes.

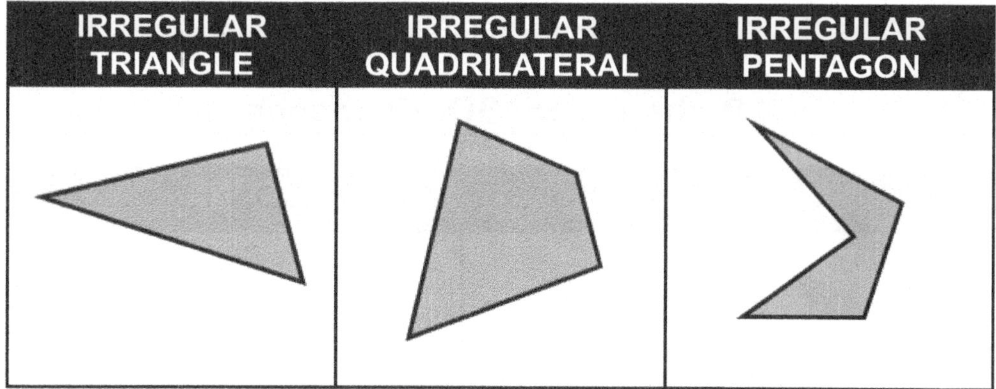

- The triangle has 3 different side lengths. Its angles would also be different.

- The quadrilateral has 4 different side lengths. Its angles would also be different.

- The pentagon has 5 different side lengths. Its angles would also be different.

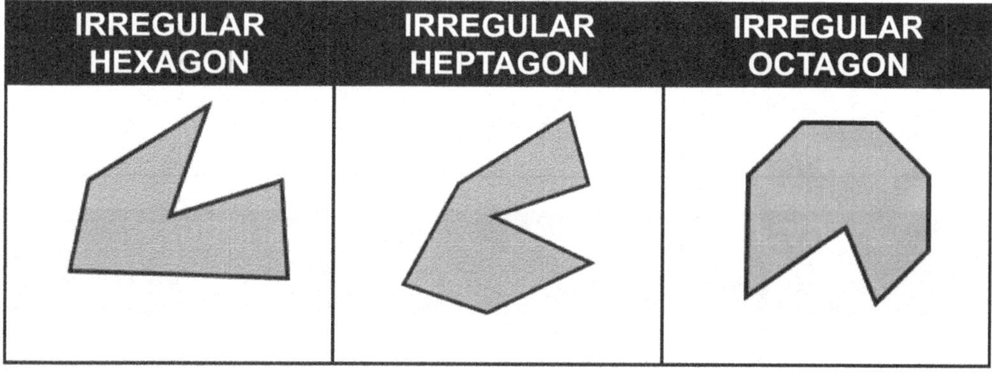

3D Shapes

3D shapes are SOLID shapes.

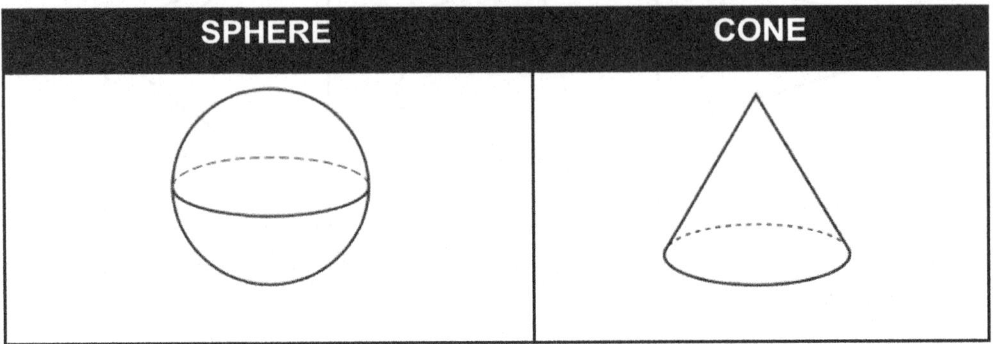

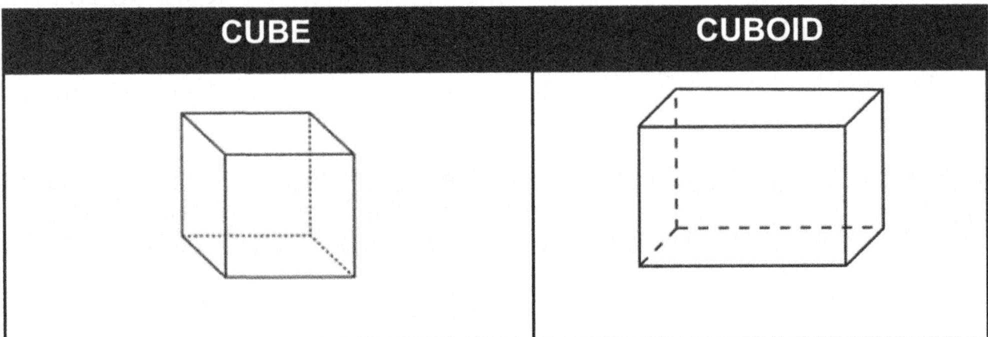

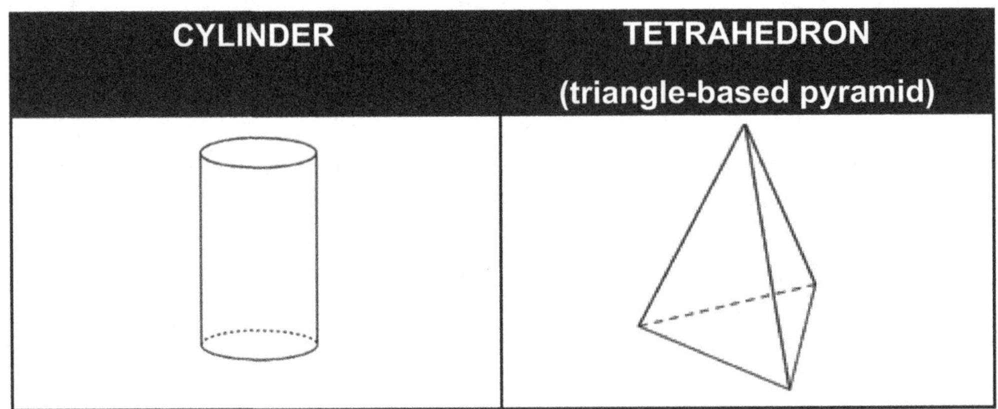

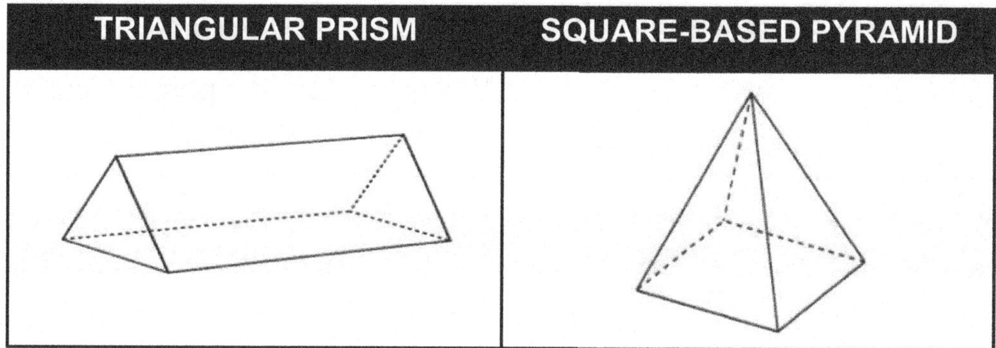

When it comes to 3D shapes, there are also some other **KEY WORDS** that you need to be aware of:

- Face

- Vertex

- Edge

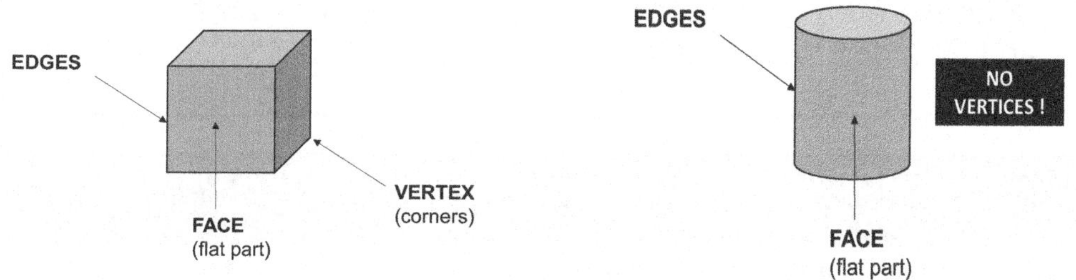

Volume of 3D Shapes

The **VOLUME** of a shape is the space inside it! The surface area of a 3D shape is the total area of ALL the faces.

VOLUME OF A CUBE AND CUBOID	VOLUME OF A PRISM
length (l) x width (w) x height (h)	area of the cross section x length (l)

VOLUME OF A CYLINDER	VOLUME OF A PYRAMID
$\pi r^2 h$ Pi x radius^2 x height (h)	$\frac{1}{3}$ x area of base x perpendicular height

VOLUME OF A CONE	VOLUME OF A SPHERE
$\frac{1}{3}\pi r^2 h$	$\frac{4}{3}\pi r^3$

Surface Area of 3D Shapes

The **SURFACE AREA** of a shape is the sum of the areas of ALL the faces.

SURFACE AREA OF A CUBE AND CUBOID	SURFACE AREA OF A CYLINDER
Find the area of each face and then add them together.	$2\pi r^2 + 2\pi rh$

SURFACE AREA OF A PYRAMID	SURFACE AREA OF A CONE
Add the area of the base to the sum of the areas of the triangular faces.	$\pi r^2 + 2\pi rl$

Circles, Sectors, and Arcs

When it comes to circles, there are a lot of tricky words to get your head around!

RADIUS, DIAMETER AND CIRCUMFERENCE

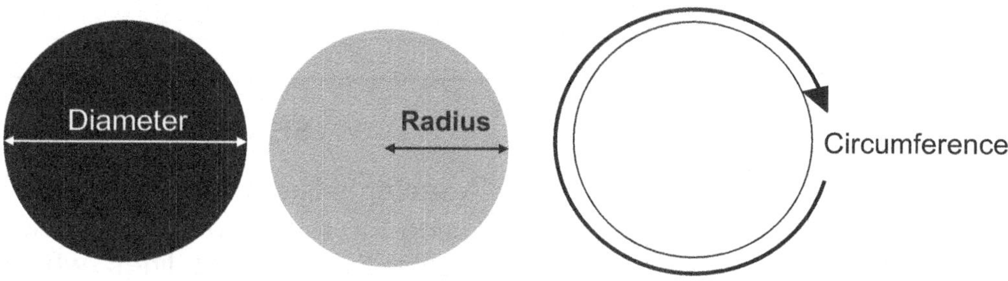

DIAMETER

The distance running right through the centre of the circle, from one side of the circle, to the other. This is twice the size of the radius.

RADIUS

The radius is half the length of the diameter.

Starting from the middle of the circle, the radius reaches the edge of the circle.

CIRCUMFERENCE

The circumference is the outer edge of a circle. Circumference = π x diameter.

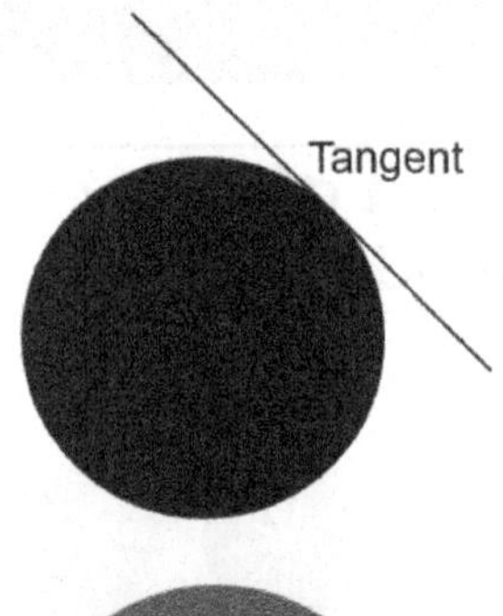

TANGENT

A tangent is a straight line which touches the outer side of the circle.

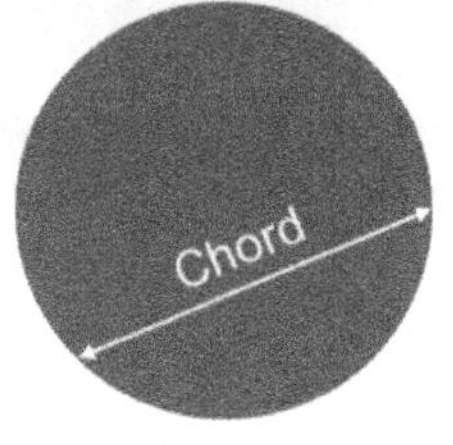

CHORD

A chord is a straight line drawn across the inside of a circle, but DOES NOT run through the centre.

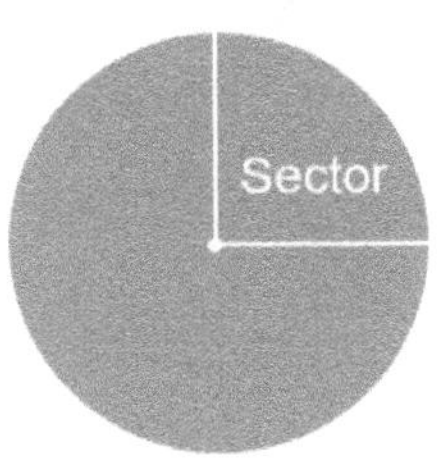

SECTOR

A sector is like a 'piece' or 'slice'. Using the mid-point of the circle, create two straight lines which reach the edge of the circle. Sector area = angle $\div$ 360° x πr^2.

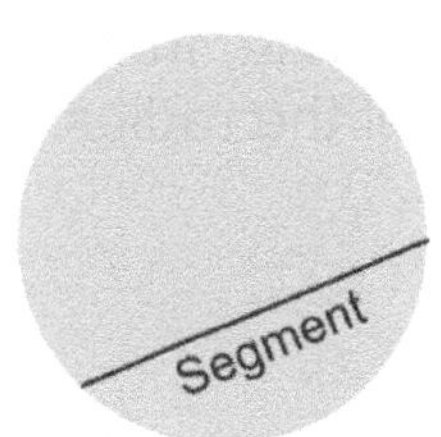

SEGMENT

A segment is the area you get when you draw a chord. The chord is the line, whereas the segment is the area in that chord.

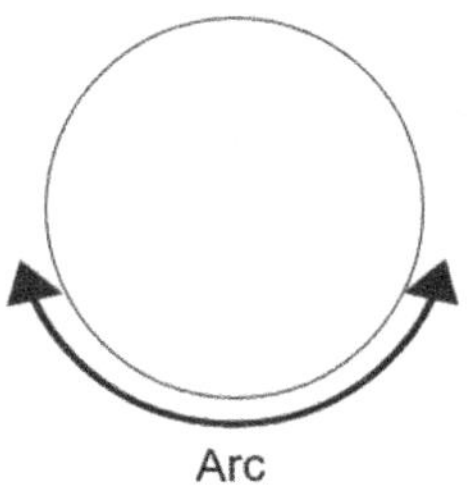

ARC

An arc is part of the circumference of the circle. Arc length = angle $\div$ 360° x πd.

Algebraic Expressions

When it comes to algebra, letters and/or symbols can be used to represent numbers.

TERM = this is a number or letter on its own.

- x x^2 $8x^3$

EXPRESSION = an expression is when terms are used alongside operations WITHOUT an equals sign.

- $3x - 2$ $xy - x$

EQUATION = an equation is when terms are used alongside operations WITH an equals sign.

- $3x + 4 = 10$

Simplifying Expressions

Simplifying expressions, also known as collecting "like" terms, allows you to make the expression easier to read.

EXAMPLE

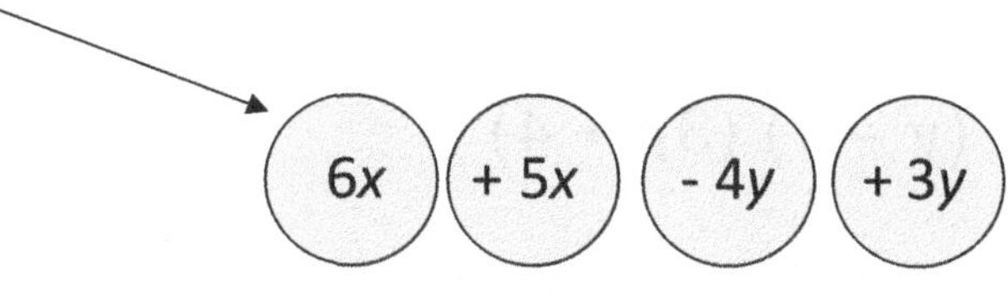

Using the expression in the above example, you can see that there are two different expressions - the terms that have the letter '*x*', and the terms that have the letter '*y*'.

That means we can simplify the expression as follows:

- The '*x*' terms can be collected together to give 11x.

- The '*y*' terms can be collected together to give -1y.

Expanding Brackets

Multiplying brackets is quite a tricky thing to get your head around.

<u>There are a few things that you can learn to make your life easier when it comes to multiplying out brackets:</u>

1. The most important thing to remember is that everything **INSIDE** the bracket should be multiplied by the term (or number) **OUTSIDE** of the bracket.

2. If there is a minus sign **OUTSIDE** of the bracket, that will **REVERSE** all of the signs when multiplying.

EXAMPLE 1

$$3(a + b) + 2(a + b)$$

- $(3a + 3b) + (2a + 2b)$
- $5a + 5b$

EXAMPLE 2

$$(y - 1)(3y + 4)$$

- $(y \times 3y) + (y \times 4) + (-1 \times 3y) + (-1 \times 4)$

    3y²   **+ 4y**   **-3y**   **-4**

- $3y^2 + 1y - 4$

Factorization

Factorizing is the process of putting brackets back in to expressions.

EXAMPLE

Factorize:

$$4y - 8$$

<u>How to factorize:</u>

* First of all, you need to find the highest common factor. This will either be a number or term.

* The common factor will be placed outside of the bracket. The numbers and terms inside the brackets will be multiplied by the outside term.

4y - 8

* 4 and 8 are both divisible by 4. So, the number 4 will be placed outside of the brackets.

* Next, you need to work out what you need to multiply by the 4 in order to get the rest of the expression.

$$4(y - 2)$$

If you expand this answer, you should reach the expression we first started with: $4y - 8$.

Quadratic Equations

The most general way to write a quadratic equation is like so:

$$ax^2 + bx + c = 0$$

QUADRATIC EQUATIONS contain only terms up to and including x^2. In the above example, you need to remember that a cannot be equal to 0, but the terms b and c can.

QUADRATIC FORMULA

This formula can be used for equations that cannot be factorized. The formula is:

$$\frac{-b \pm \sqrt{b^2 - 4ac}}{2a}$$

EXAMPLE

Solve the following quadratic equation:

$$(x + 9)(x - 4) = 0$$

- The product of $x + 9 = 0$ OR $x - 4 = 0$.
- $x + 9 = 0$
- $x = -9$
- $x - 4 = 0$
- $x = -4$
- So, $x = -9$ or $x = -4$.

MATHEMATICS KNOWLEDGE

- Brush up on your maths vocabulary. Refresh your memory with mathematical terminology which is listed on page 84.

- Recap on your maths high school knowledge. You will be required to have a strong standard of basic mathematical concepts.

- Keep in mind the B.I.D.M.A.S technique when ordering your calculations.

- If you don't know the answer, take an educated guess. You can eliminate some of the options you know to be incorrect.

- Keep an eye on the time. Remember you only have 24 minutes to answer all 25 questions for the paper-version of the ASVAB (20 minutes to answer 16 questions on the computer-version). That works out to be around 57 seconds per question!

- As with any test, it is important to undergo in-depth revision. The only way to enhance your knowledge is to revise your basic mathematical skills. Break up your revision time using a timetable. Focus on the areas that you are not so confident with.

MATHEMATICS KNOWLEDGE

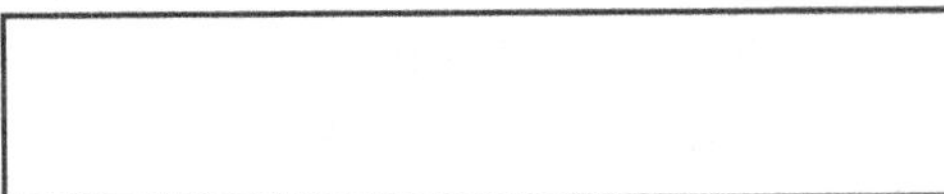

QUESTION 1

Factorize:

$$64a^2 - 81b^2$$

A. (8a - 9b) x 8

B. (8a - 9b) (8a + 9b)

C. (8a - 8b) (9a + 9b)

D. (8a - b) + 8a

QUESTION 2

Find the shaded area. Write your answer to 2 decimal places.

A. 28.27cm^2

B. 12.25cm^2

C. 144.46cm^2

D. 134.60cm^2

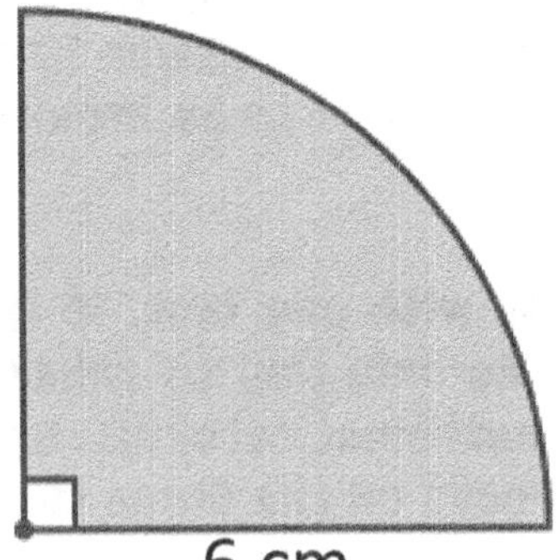

QUESTION 3

The Siberian tiger population in Country A is 60% of the Siberian tiger population in Country B. The population of Siberian tigers in Country C is 50% of that in Country A.

If the Siberian tiger population in Country C is 420, what is the Siberian tiger population in Country B?

A. 1,400

B. 1,200

C. 1,000

D. 1,600

QUESTION 4

Work out the length of side A. Give your answer correct to nearest whole number.

A. 30cm

B. 12cm

C. 14cm

D. 22cm

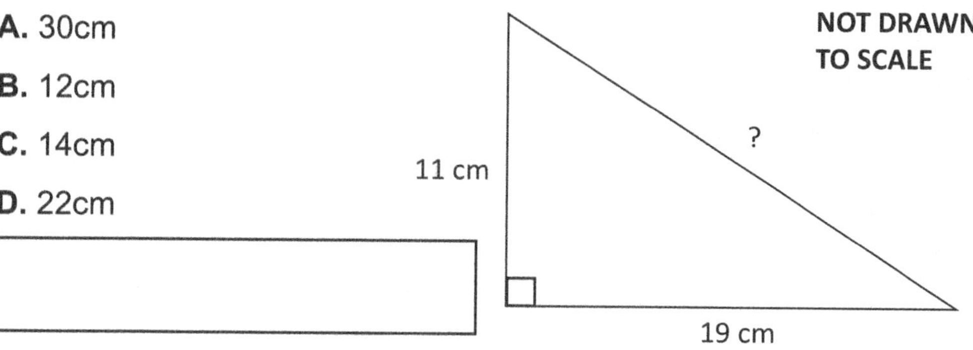

QUESTION 5

James runs from 4.50pm until 5.20pm at an average speed of 7 km/h. How far did he go?

A. 3.5 kilometers

B. 4 kilometers

C. 4.5 kilometers

D. 6 kilometers

QUESTION 6

The rule you are given is $7n + 9$.

If n represents the nth term in the sequence, what would the 35th term in the seqeunce be?

A. 320

B. 254

C. 314

D. 300

QUESTION 7

Solve the equation:

$$2(4b + 7) - 2b = 3(3b) - 10$$

A. 3

B. 4

C. 6

D. 8

QUESTION 8

Change this number from its standard index form to its actual number.

$$7.79 \times 10^{-4}$$

A. 0.000779

B. 0.79

C. 7,790,000

D. 0.779

QUESTION 9

What is the average of the following?

124, 76, 21, -6, 7

A. 111

B. 222

C. 44.4

D. 78.8

QUESTION 10

Seven burgers are vegetarian, three burgers are plain cheeseburgers, and six are cheese and bacon burgers. What is the probability that a randomly selected burger is cheese and bacon?

A. $^2/_3$

B. $^3/_8$

C. $^5/_7$

D. $^2/_7$

ANSWERS TO MATHEMATICS KNOWLEDGE PRACTICE QUESTIONS

Q1. B. (8a - 9b) (8a + 9b)

- Both 64 and 81 are square numbers.

- $(8a)^2 + (9b)^2$

- $(8a - 9b)(8a + 9b)$

Q2. A. 28.27

EXPLANATION =

- $6 \times 6 = 36$

- $36 \div 4$

- $4 \times \pi = 28.27 cm^2$

Q3. A. 1,400

EXPLANATION = Siberian tiger population in Country C is 50% of that in Country A.

If country C is 420, Country A = 420 x 100 ÷ 50 = 840.

So, if Country A = 840 and is 60% of the population in Country B, Country B = 840 x 100 ÷ 60 = 1,400.

Q4. D. 22 cm

EXPLANATION =

- $11^2 = 121$
- $19^2 = 361$
- $121 + 361 = 482$
- $\sqrt{482} = 21.95449...$
- To one decimal place = 22.0

Q5. A. 3.5 kilometers

EXPLANATION:

- 4.50 pm – 5.20pm = 30 minutes.
- 30 minutes = 0.5 hour.

* So, distance = 7 x 0.5 = 3.5 km.

Q6. B. 254

* 7 x 35 = 245

* 245 + 9 = 254

Q7. D. 8

* $8b + 14 - 2b = 9b - 10$

* $8b + 24 - 2b = 9b$

* $8b - 2b = 6b$

* $24 = 9b - 6b = 3b$

* $b = 8$

Q8. A. 0.000779

* If you have a minus number, this means that the original number will decrease, instead of increase.

* The decimal point will move four spaces to the left.

Q9. C. 44.4

EXPLANATION =

* 124 + 76 + 21 + 7 = 228

* 228 + -6 = 222

* 222 ÷ 5 = 44.4

Q10. B. $^3/_8$

* There are 16 burgers in total.

* The probability of choosing a cheese and bacon burger is $^6/_{16}$ or $^3/_8$.

Now move on to the Electronics Information subtest of the ASVAB.

ELECTRONICS INFORMATION

The Electronics Information section of the ASVAB requires you to have a basic understanding of electrical principles, radio, television, currents, engines and magnets.

During this section of your Armed Forces assessment, the number of questions and the duration you have will depend on whether you are sitting the paper-based or computer-based version.

Subtest	Computer version	Paper version	Content
Electronics Information (EI)	16 questions 8 minutes	20 questions 9 minutes	General electronic principles

PLEASE NOTE: the Electronics Information (EI) section has **NO** impact on your Armed Forces Qualification Test (AFQT) score. However, don't take this as an opportunity to relax.

The score for this subtest will be used to calculate military composite scores for job qualification basis.

Use this chapter as a mini Electronics lesson to recap on your general electrical knowledge. Below we have outlined the key areas that you should be focusing on:

VOLTS	AMPERES	OHMS	CURRENT
WATT	ELECTRONS	RESISTANCE	RESISTORS
SAFETY	SIGNAL FLOW	MAGNETS	ELECTRICAL EFFECTS
IMPEDANCE	CAPACITORS	TRANSISTOR	SYMBOLS
ENERGY TRANSFERS	UNITS OF ELECTRIC	PARTICLES	ATOMS
ELECTRICAL PRINCIPLES	PROCESS FLOW	POTENTIAL DIFFERENCE	CIRCUITS

The Electronics Information section of the ASVAB will consist of basic electronic knowledge. Brush up on these areas before attempting our practice questions.

Electronics Terminology

The electronics tests also requires you to learn some electronics terminology.

See **APPENDIX C** for a list of terminology that you should familiarize yourself with before attempting the test of this chapter.

Electrical Symbols

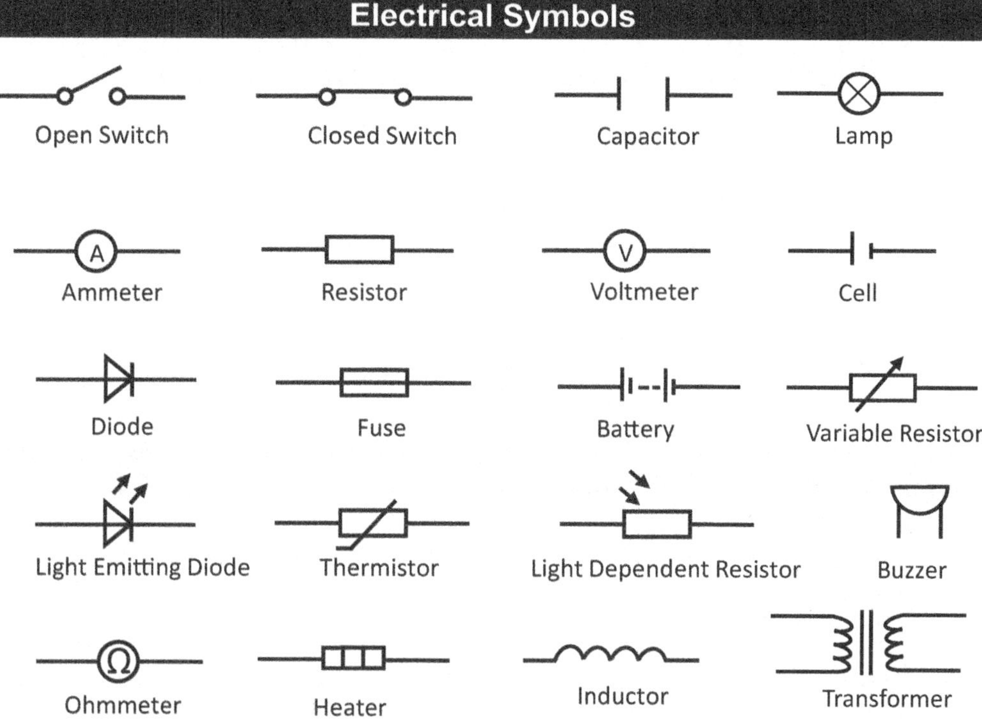

Electrical Calculations

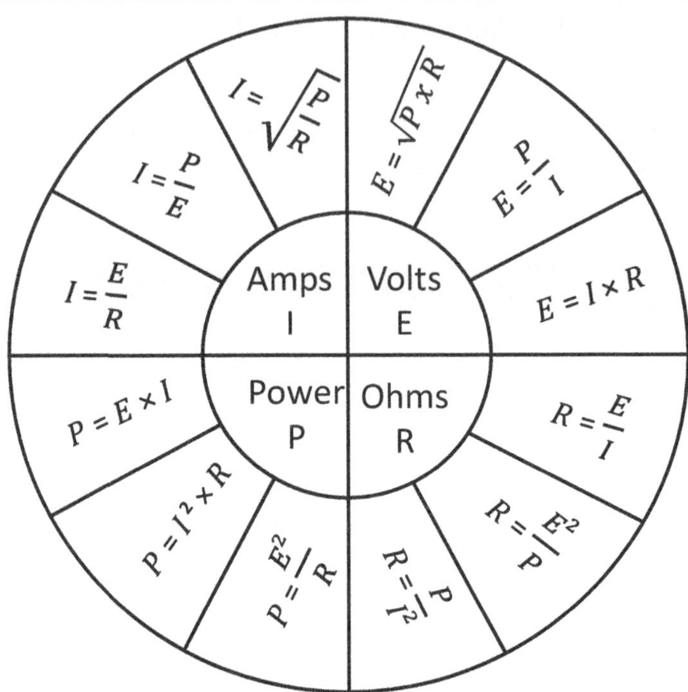

Atoms and Particles

Everything is made up of atoms. Atoms comprise of three particles:

- Protons;

- Neutrons;

- Electrons.

Neutrons – neutral.

Protons and electrons – electrically charged. Protons are positive, and electrons are negative.

The number of protons in an atom is called its 'atomic number'. The total number of electrons in an atom is the same number of the total number of protons in the nucleus. This means that atoms have no overall electrical charge. The nucleus is part of the atom that the particles surround.

Electrical Hazards

Electricity is a form of energy. You need to be fully aware of the dangers involved when using electrical components.

Below is a list of examples of ways in which you can be electrocuted if you are not careful when handling electricity:

- Pushing objects into plug sockets;

- Water touching an electrical compliance;

- Damaged wiring;

- Incorrect wiring;

- Overheated cables and plug sockets;

- Frayed cables.

Currents

AC Electricity

Alternating currents (AC) can be defined through the changes in direction which the flow of electricity undertakes.

DC Electricity

Direct currents (DC) can be established if the current flows in one direction. For example, batteries and solar cells supply direct currents, with a typical battery supplying 1.5V.

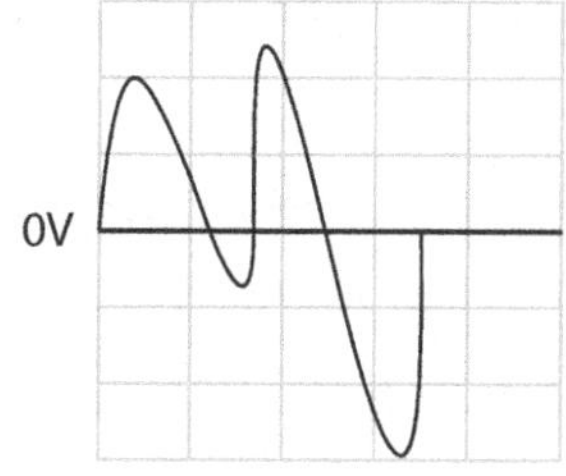

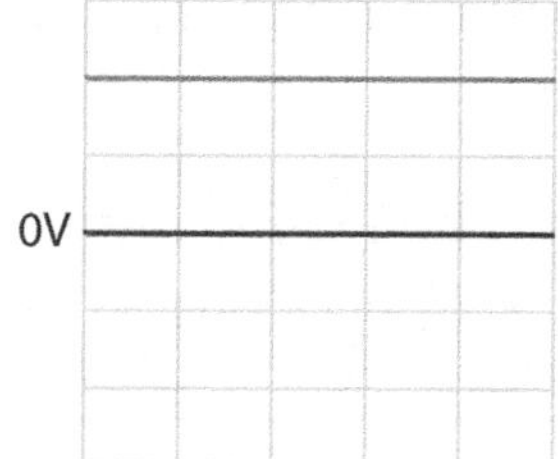

Voltages

Voltage is also known as the potential difference or electromotive force (e.m.f.). The potential difference is needed to make an electrical current flow through an electrical component. For example, cells and batteries are often used to provide the potential difference needed in a circuit.

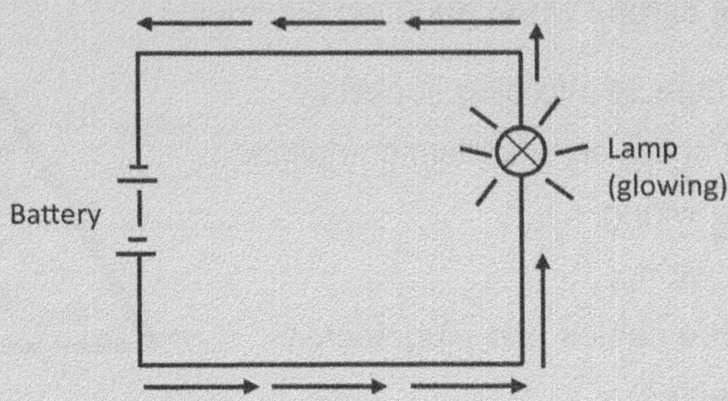

In the above electrical circuit, you will notice that there is only one source of potential difference (the battery). There is also only one source of resistance (the lamp).

Resistance

The term resistance refers to an electrical element that measures its opposition to a current. A resistance to the flow of electricity in a circuit occurs in most conductors.

The resistance of a wire can be increased in two ways:

* Increasing the length of the wire;

* Decreasing the thickness of the wire.

The resistance of a **long** wire is greater than the resistance of a **short** wire. This is because the electrons collide more with ions as it passes through.

The resistance in a **thin** wire is greater than that of the resistance of a **thick** wire. This is because a thin wire has fewer electrons to carry the current flow.

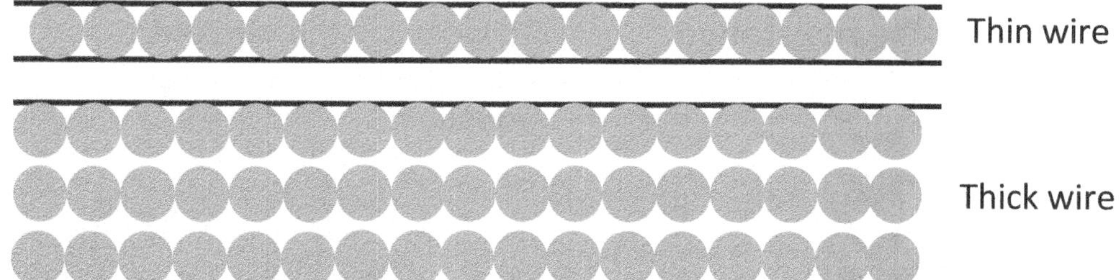

Ohm's Law

Ohm's law is often used to analyse the electrical components within a circuit. In simple terms, Ohm's law specifically focuses on three electrical concepts:

- Potential difference (voltage);
- Current;
- Resistance.

The resistance of an electrical outlet can be found by measuring the current flow and the potential difference, i.e. the voltage running through it.

There is a simple equation to use in order to work out the relationship between current, resistance and potential difference.

REMEMBER the following equation:

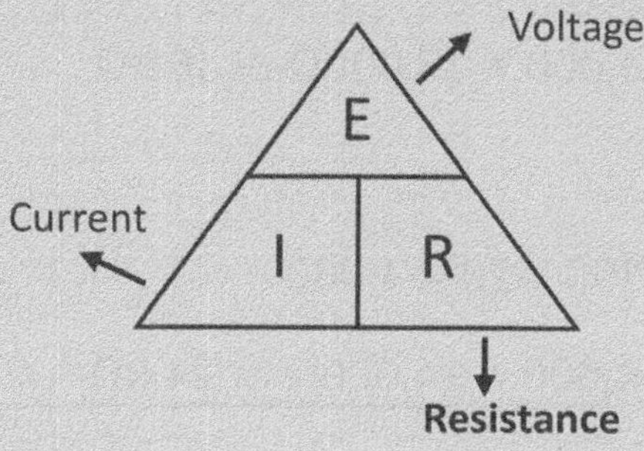

To work out the **resistance,** eliminate the 'R' from the equation:

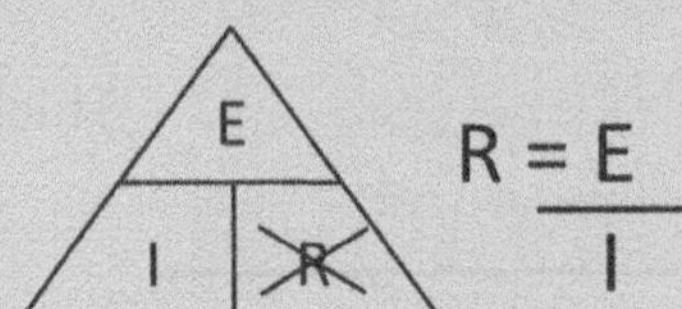

$$R = \frac{E}{I}$$

To work out the **current,** eliminate the 'I' from the equation:

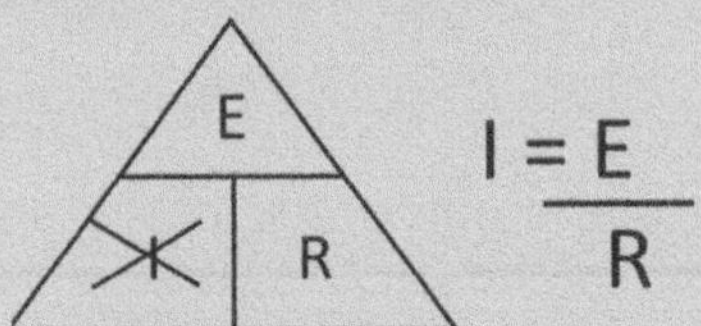

$$I = \frac{E}{R}$$

To work out the **voltage,** eliminate the 'E' from the equation:

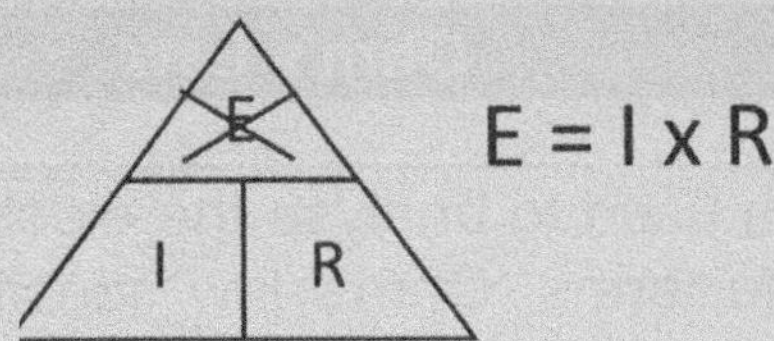

$$E = I \times R$$

Resistance Tolerance

In order to work out the minimum and maximum resistance tolerable of a resistor, you would need to use the following method:

EXAMPLE

What are the minimum and maximum acceptable values if a resistor has the resistance of 20 kΩ and can tolerate ±20%?

Minimum value

Step 1 – 20,000 ÷ 100 x 20 = 4,000.

Step 2 – 20,000 – 4,000 = 16,000Ω or 16 kΩ

Maximum value

Step 1 – 20,000 ÷ 100 x 20 = 4,000.

Step 2 – 20,000 + 4,000 = 24,000Ω or 24 kΩ

ELECTRONICS INFORMATION

- Having a basic understanding of physics and electronics will be an advantage. You need to feel fully equipped to tackle the questions and score highly on the assessment. Brush up on the basics of physics, circuits and electronics.

- It is important that you learn and practice the different types of electrical questions that you are likely to encounter on the job. Work out what types of electrical knowledge are required for the job in which you are applying, and focus your preparation around these areas.

- If you don't know the answer, take an educated guess. You can eliminate some of the options you know to be incorrect.

- Keep an eye on the time. Remember you only have 9 minutes to answer all 20 questions for the paper-version of the ASVAB (8 minutes to answer 16 questions on the computer-version). That works out to be around 25 seconds per question!

- As with any test, it is important to undergo in-depth revision. The only way to enhance your knowledge is to revise your basic electrical skills. Break up your revision time using a timetable. Focus on the areas that you are not so confident with.

ELECTRONICS INFORMATION

QUESTION 1

An atom's atomic number is determined by the number of what?

A. Neutrons.

B. Protons.

C. Electrons.

D. Atoms.

QUESTION 2

What happens when an electrical charge flows through a resistor?

A. The temperature decreases.

B. The temperature increases.

C. The temperature fluctuates.

D. The temperature stays the same.

QUESTION 3

Which of the following bests describes the function of a green and yellow striped wire in a plug?

A. Completes the circuit.

B. Carries high voltage.

C. A safety wire that prevents the appliance from becoming 'live'.

D. None of the above.

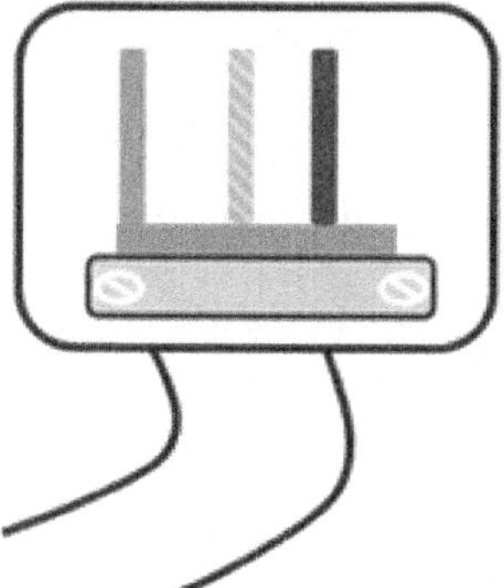

QUESTION 4

Why does a vacuum cleaner not contain an earth wire?

A. They have plastic casings which gives you an electric shock.

B. The charge is not enough to get electrocuted.

C. They have plastic casings which stops you getting an electric shock.

D. None of the above.

QUESTION 5

________ are a form of wasteful circulation currents which are observed in iron cores, which result in loss of energy.

A. Core currents.

B. Hysteresis currents.

C. Neutral currents.

D. Eddy currents.

QUESTION 6

Which of the following words best describes the explanation:

The opposite to current flow found in an alternating current circuit and is often labelled with the symbol 'Z'.

A. Inertial force.

B. Work done.

C. Impedance.

D. Step up transformers.

QUESTION 7

Which of the following explanations best describes the function of an RCD (residual current device)?

A. A flow of electricity along an unintended path in the circuit.

B. A safety device that stops electricity passing through if there is a fault.

C. A point in a wiring system where devices can be connected.

D. A way to measure the current flowing through alternating current circuits.

QUESTION 8

What would happen if a copper conductor was moved across a magnetic field?

A. The wire would become magnetic.

B. A current would be instigated into the wire.

C. The conductor would remain unaffected.

D. A voltage would be instigated into the wire.

QUESTION 9

The Wheatstone bridge circuit below is balanced, with R2 = 40 Ω, R3 = 20 Ω and R4 = 80 Ω. What is the value of R1?

A. 5 Ω

B. 20Ω

C. 10Ω

D. 40Ω

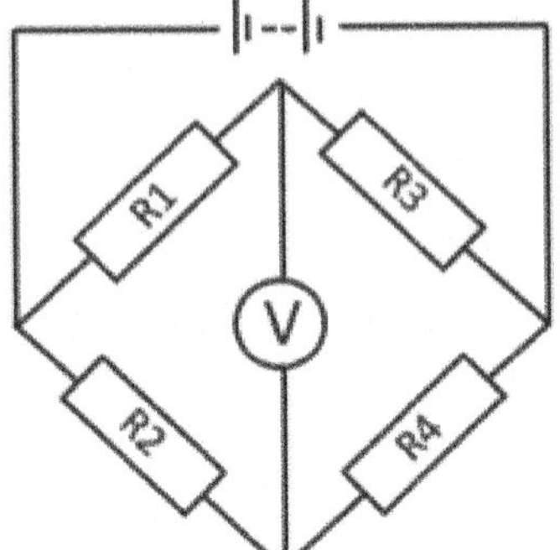

QUESTION 10

The main component in analogue electronics is __________

A. Fuse.

B. Transformer.

C. Op-amp.

D. Thermistor.

ANSWERS TO ELECTRONICS INFORMATION PRACTICE QUESTIONS

Q1. B. Protons

EXPLANATION = an atomic number is determined by the number of protons in an atom's nucleus.

Q2. B. The temperature increases

EXPLANATION = when an electrical charge flows through a resistor, the temperature increases. The resister gets hot from the electrical charge running through it, therefore increasing the temperature.

Q3. C. A safety wire that prevents the appliance from becoming 'live'

EXPLANATION = the green and yellow striped wire i.e. the 'earth' wire in a plug is used as a safety wire that prevents the appliance from being 'live' and thus prevents an electrical shock. The blue wire is the 'neutral' wire that completes the circuit, and the brown wire is the 'live' wire that carries a high voltage within the electrical circuit.

Q4. C. They have plastic casings which stop you getting an electric shock.

EXPLANATION = vacuums have plastic castings which stop you getting an electric shock.

Q5. D. Eddy currents

EXPLANATION = Eddy currents lose energy due to the changes in magnetic fields in a conductor or core.

Q6. C. Impedance

EXPLANATION = impedance is the total opposite of the current flow in an alternating current circuit, and is labelled Z. An impedance is a way to measure the ratio between the voltage and the current in an alternating current circuit.

Q7. B. A safety device that stops electricity passing through if there is a fault

EXPLANATION = an RCD (residual current device) is a safety device that stops electricity passing through if there is a fault.

Q8. D. A voltage would be instigated into the wire

EXPLANATION = a voltage can be induced into the wire if the copper conductor is moved across a magnetic field. Some of the electrons are free and therefore contain a force. The electrons are pushed downwards which leaves behind a positive charge. The electrons are negatively charged, so the charge in the wire has become separated which causes a voltage.

Q9. C = 10 Ω

EXPLANATION = in order to work out the value of R1, you should use the following method:

Step 1 = R1 ÷ R2 = R3 ÷ R4.

Step 2 = R1 ÷ 40 = 20 ÷ 80 = 0.25

Step 3 = So, we need to find the value of R1 that once divided by 40, would give you 0.25.

Step 4 = 20 x 40 ÷ 80 = 10.

Step 5 = to make sure that you have the correct answer, you can double check that the value you have, gives you 0.25. So, 10 ÷ 40 = 0.25. Therefore, 10 would be the correct answer.

Q10. C = op-amp

EXPLANATION = the main component of analogue electronics is an op-amp. Analogue electronics uses signals which are constantly changing to determine the physical quality of something i.e. to measure the loudness of a sound. This is measured using an operational amplifier (op-amp).

Now move on to the Auto and Shop Information subtest of the ASVAB.

AUTO AND SHOP INFORMATION

The Auto and Shop Information section of the ASVAB requires you to have a basic understanding of automative systems and repairs. You will also be required to have a strong knowledge of various shop tools.

During this section of your Armed Forces assessment, the number of questions and the duration you have for this section will depend on whether you are sitting the paper-based or computer-based version.

Subtest	Computer version	Paper version	Content
Auto & Shop Information (AS)	22 questions 13 minutes	25 questions 11 minutes	Knowledge of tools and automobiles

PLEASE NOTE: the Auto and Shop Information (AS) section has **NO** impact on your Armed Forces Qualification Test (AFQT) score. However, don't take this as an opportunity to relax.

The score for this subtest will be used to calculate military composite scores for job qualification basis.

Use this chapter as a mini lesson to recap on your general auto shop knowledge. Below we have outlined the key areas that you should be focusing on:

ENGINES	OCTANE RATINGS	COOLING SYSTEM	ELECTRICAL SYSTEMS
IGNITION SYSTEMS	DRIVE SYSTEM	BRAKE SYSTEM	FILTERS
STRIKING TOOLS	FASTENING TOOLS	CUTTING TOOLS	CLAMPING TOOLS
FINISHING TOOLS	MEASURING TOOLS	GOUGING TOOLS	LEVELING TOOLS
SQUARING TOOLS	SCREWS	BOLTS	NUTS AND WASHERS

Auto and Shop Terminology

The Auto and Shop subtest of the ASVAB has a lot of complicated terminology for you to learn and understand.

See **APPENDIX D** for a list of terminology that you should familiarize yourself with before attempting the rest of this chapter.

Car Engines

FOUR STROKE CYCLE ENGINE

Intake	Fuel and air are filtered through the carburetor into the piston as the intake valve opens.
Compression	The valves close and the connecting rod pushes up the piston which compresses the gas and air.
Power	After the gas and air are compressed, it needs a spark. The ignition coil creates high voltage in the spark plug, and once the mixture is lit, the hot air pushes the piston back down the cylinder.
Exhaust	The exhuast valve opens as the piston pushes the gas out the chamber. The valve then closes and the intake valve opens again in order to repeat the whole cycle.

Car Cooling System

When a car engine is running, it produces a lot of heat. In order for the engine to run efficiently, without melting, the engine needs to be cooled.

Generally speaking, a car is cooled down by a coolant liquid (water mixed with antifreeze). This prevents the engine from overheating. Other car engines are cooled down by air flowing over finned cylinder casings.

Water-Cooled Cooling System	Water-cooled cooling systems contain a block and cylinder which have coolant channels running through them. Unwanted heat is passed from the radiator and cooled liquid returns to an inlet.
Air-Cooled Cooling System	Air-cooled cooling systems contain a block and cylinder which are made with deep fins on the outside.
Fan	A fan is used to help the airflow and prevent the engine from overheating when the car is stationary.

Car Driving System

Front-Wheel Drive	A transmission driving system that provides power to the front wheels of a vehicle.
Rear-Wheel Drive	A transmission driving system that provides power to the rear wheels of a vehicle.
All-Wheel Drive (Four-Wheel Drive)	A transmission driving system that provides torque to all its wheels at the same time.

Car Braking Systems

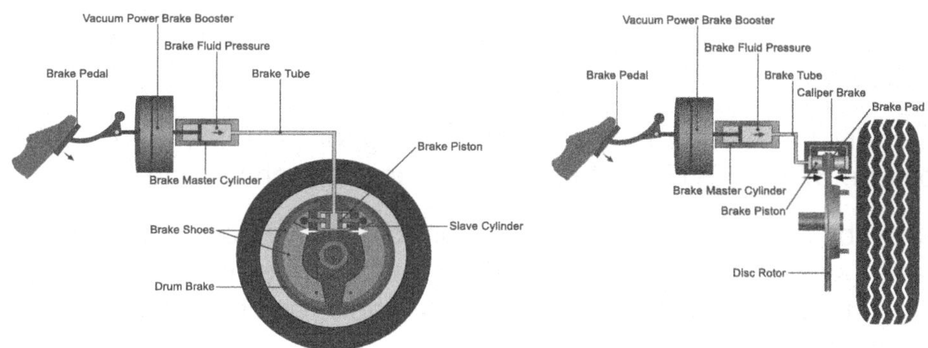

Car Emissions-Control Systems

Air-Injection System	A system that forces air into the exhaust system to burn fuel before it comes out of the exhaust pipe.
Catalytic Converter	Oxidize carbon monoxide and hydrocarbons into water vapour and carbon dioxide.
Exhaust-Gas-Recirculation System	Controls nitrogen-oxide emissions by forcing some gases back into the cylinders.
Positive-Crankcase Ventilation	An older method (although still used) that forces unburned fuel back into the cylinder so that it can be burned.

Octane Ratings

Octane rating is a measurement used to determine a fuel's ability to resist 'knock'. By 'knock', we mean a rattling or pinging sound which is a result of premature ignition.

The higher the octane number, the greater the fuel's resistance to knocking.

Generally, the recommended octane rating for the majority of vehicles is octane 87 (in the U.S.), but this will vary to each vehicle.

You will be able to work out whether or not your vehicle has the correct octane level by listening to how your car sounds. If it doesn't knock when you use the recommended octane, then you are using the correct amount of gasoline.

Striking Tools

Sledge	A sledgehammer is a large, flat, often metal head, attached to a handle. It is used to break rock.
Hammer	A hammer is a tool with a heavy metal head used for driving in nails and breaking things.
Mallet	A mallet can be made from metal, plastic, wood, rubber or rawhide. This is used to strike another tool or surface without damaging it.

Fastening Tools

Allen Wrench	A tool to drive bolts and screws with hexagonal sockets in their heads.
Box Wrench	A wrench with a closed socket that covers over a nut or bolt head.
Cutting Pliers	A tool used to cut material such as wire.
Curved-Nose Pliers	A tool used to cut and hold material. Used to bend, re-position, or snip.
Long-Nosed Pliers	A tool used to cut and hold material. Used to bend, re-position, or snip.
Offset Screwdriver	A screwdriver with a blade at a right angle to the shaft.
Open-End Wrench	A wrench with jaws having a fixed width of opening at one or both ends.
Phillips Screwdriver	A screwdriver that has a cross-shaped tip.
Pipe Wrench	A tool used for turning soft pipes and fittings with a rounded surface.
Pliers	Pincers used for gripping or bending wire.
Slip-Joint Pliers	Pliers with a pivot point that can be altered to increase the size range of the jaws.
Socket Wrench	A ratchet tool with a series of detachable sockets for tightening and loosening nuts.
Standard Screwdriver	A tool used for turning a screw. This type of screwdriver will have a long, flat head.
Stapler	A device used for fastening objects together with the use of staples.
Torque Wrench	A tool used for setting and adjusting the tightness of nuts and bolts.
Wrench	A tool used to turn something.
Wrench Pliers	A tool with derrated jaws that clamp objects.

Cutting Tools

Bolt Cutters	When the handles are closed, the shears are able to slice through metal objects.
Circle Snips	Circle snips are used to cut curves.
Coping Saw	Coping saws are a type of handsaw that is used to cut shapes or curved lines.
Crosscut Saw	Crosscut saws are a type of handsaw that cuts against the grain of wood.
Hacksaw	A hacksaw is used to cut metal.
Pipe Cutters / Tube Cutters	This is a type of cutter that is used to score and cut metal objects.
Ripsaw	A ripsaw is a type of handsaw that cuts against the grain of wood.
Snips and Shears	Snips and shears have cutting blades (like scissors) which can be used to cut curved or straight.

Chisels

Metal-Cutting Chisels	Chisels that are able to cut into metal. Usually struck with a mallet.
Wood-Cutting Chisels	Chisels that are able to cut into wood. Socket chisels are struck with a mallet to cut through wood. Other chisels require only pressure from your hands.

Drills

Auger Bits	Auger bits pierce large holes.
Countersink	Countersink is a drill which enlarges the surface of a hole so a screw can be inserted.
Twist Drills	Twist drills are used to create holes.

Clamping Tools

Bench Vise	A vise with large jaws which holds material in place.
Clamps	Used when a vise doesn't work. Clamps generally connect to the items (not on a bench)
Handscrew Vise	A vise with two jaws connected by screws. The screws are used to tighten the vise together.
Pipe Vise	A vise that holds round pipes or trims.
Pliers	Pliers can be used to hold objects.
Vises	Hold material while being sawed, drilled or glued.

Finishing Tools

Double-Cut	Double cut files are used for rough work.
Flat Files and Half-Round	Files that are used for general purposes.
Single-Cut	Files that are used for finishing work and sharpening blades.
Square and Round	Files fit square and/or round openings.

Measuring Tools

Calipers	Calipers are used for very small and exact measurements.
Depth Gauges	Depth gauges measure the depths of holes.
Tape Rules	Tape rules are used to measure material.
Level	Levels are a tool which allows you to place it on a surface to see if the surface is level.
Square Level	A square level is used to check the accuracy of an angle.
Thickness Gauges	Thickness gauges measure the thickness of holes.
Wire Gauges	Wire gauges measure the thickness of wire.

Fastening Bits

Bolts	Bolts are flat ended and are held in place by a nut and washer.
Brads and Finishing Nails	These type of nails have heads which are made to fit in line or slighly below the surface of wood.
Common Nails	These are nails that are used for general purposes.
Double-Headed Nails	This type of nail has two heads, one lower than the other. The nail is driven into an object until it reaches the lower head, but can be pulled out by the higher head.
Lag Screws	Lag screws have square or hexagonal shaped heads.
Machine Screws	Machine screws are used for metal. They come in various sizes and have a variety of different heads.
Nuts	Nuts can come in different shapes. They can be square or hexagonal. Cap nuts are round and smooth. Stop nuts prevent screws or bolts from coming loose. Wing nuts have 'wings' on each side so they can be tightened by hand.
Rivets	Rivets are used to fasten metal objects together.
Washers	Washers prevent damage to a surface by preventing the bolt from digging into the materia.
Wood Screws	Wood screws are used to fasten wood objects together.

AUTO AND SHOP INFORMATION

QUICK TIPS

- You will need to have a good understanding with regards to functioning vehicles, shop practices and equipment, tools and functions, and much more.

- The auto and shop information subtest is probably the one you will be least familiar with. Reading car manuals, taking a college course, researching online and talking to people with experience are all ways to improve your knowledge in this area.

- If you don't know the answer, take an educated guess. You can eliminate some of the options you know to be incorrect.

- Keep an eye on the time. Remember you only have 11 minutes to answer all 25 questions for the paper-version of the ASVAB (13 minutes to answer 22 questions on the computer-version). That works out to be around 26 seconds per question!

- As with any test, it is important to undergo in-depth revision. The only way to enhance your knowledge is to revise your basic automotor skills. Break up your revision time using a timetable. Focus on the areas that you are not so confident with.

AUTO AND SHOP INFORMATION

QUESTION 1

Which of the following should be tightened by hand?

A. Bolt.

B. Machine screw.

C. Wing nut.

D. Wood screw.

QUESTION 2

What is it called if you make a hole wider than half an inch?

A. Screwing.

B. Drilling.

C. Boring.

D. Nailing.

QUESTION 3

Which tool would be best to use to chip or cut wood?

A. Butt chisel.

B. Depth gauge.

C. Augur bit.

D. Thread gauge.

QUESTION 4

Why are clean air filters important?

A. Clean filters helps with the cooling system.

B. Dirty filters can decrease in mile fuelage.

C. Dirty filters can decrease engine performance.

D. Both B and C.

QUESTION 5

If a car has a fuel injection system, which of the following will the car NOT need?

A. Oil filter.

B. Carburetor.

C. Tachometer.

D. Drum brakes.

QUESTION 6

What is the role of an air-injected system?

A. To force air into the exhaust system to burn fuel before it leaves the exhaust pipe.

B. To force air into the water vapour to prevent unwanted pollutants.

C. To force air into the cylinder so that fuel can be burned.

D. None of the above.

QUESTION 7

Which of the following best defines 'Torque'?

A. To prevent pollutants from poisoning the atmosphere.

B. To stop the wheels from rotating.

C. Varies the amount of power to the engine.

D. The force that produces wheel rotation.

QUESTION 8

A valve is used to perform which of the following tasks?

A. Control the flow of a liquid.

B. Increase the temperature of a liquid.

C. Facilitate the evaporation of a liquid.

D. Decrease the density of a liquid.

QUESTION 9

When an aeroplane is being refuelled, to avoid causing a spark which could build up from static charge…

A. The person pouring in the fuel needs to pour it in slowly.

B. The aeroplane has rubber tyres which insulates the charges.

C. The refuelling tank and the aeroplane itself are earthed.

D. The person pouring in the fuel needs to pour it in fast.

QUESTION 10

Which spanner will it be harder to tighten the bolt with?

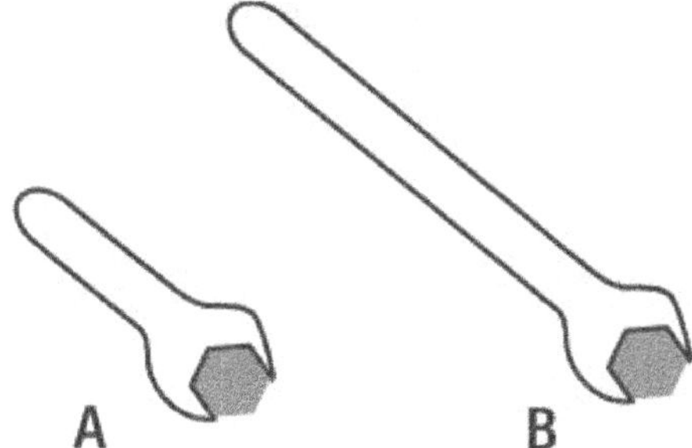

A. Spanner A

B. Spanner B.

C. Both the same.

D. It is the wrong tool to tighten up the bolt.

ANSWERS TO AUTO AND SHOP INFORMATION PRACTICE QUESTIONS

Q1. C. Wing nut

Q2. C. Boring

Q3. A. Butt chisel

Q4. D. Both B and C

Q5. B. Carburetor

Q6. A. To force air into the exhaust system to burn fuel before it leaves the exhaust pipe

Q7. D. The force that produces wheel rotation

Q8. A. Control the flow of a liquid

Q9. C. The refuelling tank and the aeroplane itself are earthed

Q10. A. Spanner A

Now move on to the Mechanical Comprehension subtest of the ASVAB.

MECHANICAL COMPREHENSION

The Mechanical Comprehension section of the ASVAB requires you to have a basic high school knowledge of mechanical concepts.

During this section of your Armed Forces assessment, the number of questions and the duration you have for this section will depend on whether you are sitting the paper-based or computer-based version.

Subtest	Computer version	Paper version	Content
Mechanical Comprehension (MC)	16 questions 20 minutes	25 questions 19 minutes	Basic mechanical knowledge

PLEASE NOTE: the Mechanical Comprehension (MC) section has **NO** impact on your Armed Forces Qualification Test (AFQT) score. However, don't take this as an opportunity to relax.

The score for this subtest will be used to calculate military composite scores for job qualification basis.

Use this chapter as a mini lesson to recap on your general mechanical knowledge. Below we have outlined the key areas that you should be focusing on:

LEVERS	PULLEYS	GEARS	SPRINGS
ELECTRICAL CIRCUITS	TOOLS	FORCES	RESISTANCE
POWER	MECHANICAL ADVANTAGE	BLOCK AND TACKLE	INCLINED PLANE
BELT SYSTEMS	VISES	HYDRAULIC JACK	EFFORT

Pulleys

If the pulley is fixed, then the force required is equal to the weight. A simple way to work out how to calculate the force that is required, is to divide the weight by the number of sections of rope supporting it.

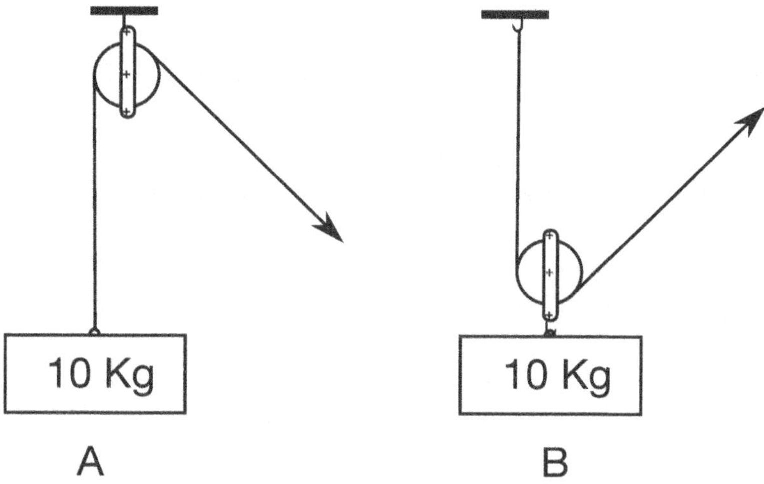

DIAGRAM A = there is only one section of rope supporting the weight, therefore this can be worked out by = 10 ÷ 1 = 10.

DIAGRAM B = there are two ropes supporting the weight, therefore this can be worked out by: 10 (weight) ÷ 2 (number of ropes supporting the weight) = 5.

Springs

When springs are arranged in a series, each spring can be the subject of the force applied. If the springs are arranged in a parallel line, the force is divided equally between them.

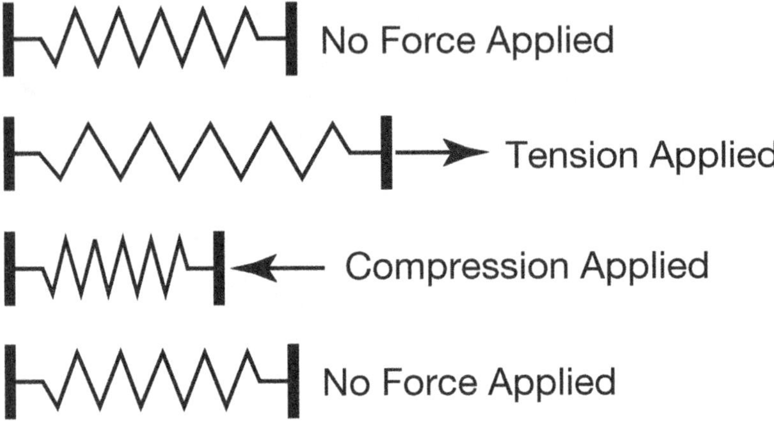

Gears

If gears are connected by a chain or belt, then the gears will all move in the same direction.

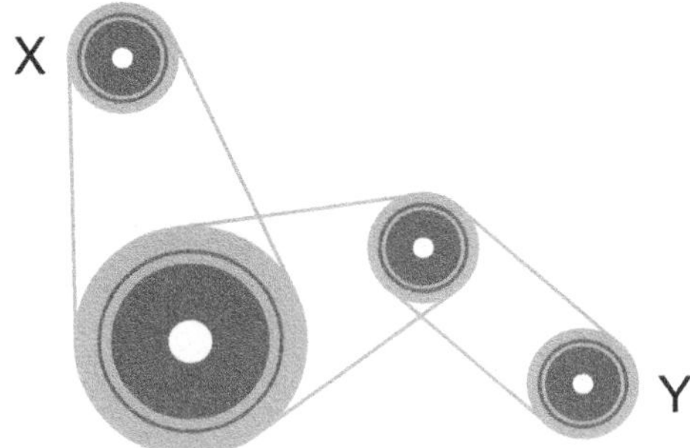

If the gears are touching (as shown in the example below), then adjacent gears move in the opposite direction. In the example, X and Y will move in opposite directions.

Circuits

Questions regarding circuits usually follow a similar circuit, which will include: a power source, switches, bulbs and a path of wiring.

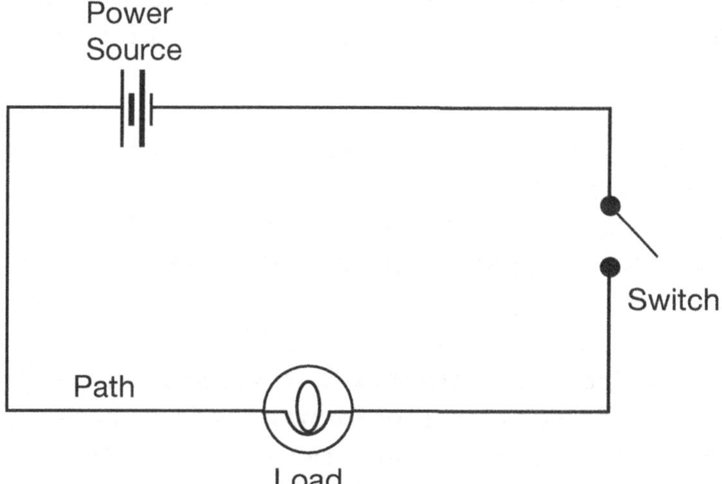

MECHANICAL COMPREHENSIÓN

QUICK TIPS

- You will need to have a good understanding of Mechanical Comprehension. For topics to revise, see page 166.

- In the build-up to the test, if you feel like you are struggling with basic mechanical concepts, then we recommend you study a car manual.

- If you don't know the answer, take an educated guess. You can eliminate some of the options you know to be incorrect.

- Keep an eye on the time. Remember you only have 19 minutes to answer all 25 questions for the paper-version of the ASVAB (20 minutes to answer 16 questions on the computer-version). That works out to be around 45 seconds per question!

- As with any test, it is important to undergo in-depth revision. The only way to enhance your knowledge is to revise your basic mechanical skills. Break up your revision time using a timetable. Focus on the areas that you are not so confident with.

MECHANICAL COMPREHENSION

QUESTION 1

Fossil fuels are a useful way to generate power. Which of the following is NOT needed in order to produce electrical power from a fossil fuel?

A. Heat.

B. Steam.

C. Dam.

D. Turbine.

QUESTION 2

A thick block of wood rests on an even and level surface. What mechanical principle makes it more difficult to push this block sideways if the surface is made of sandpaper than if it is made of glass?

A. Spring Force

B. Gravitational Force

C. Air Resistance Force

D. Frictional Force

QUESTION 3

How far from the balance point should the 30 kg weight be placed to balance the beam?

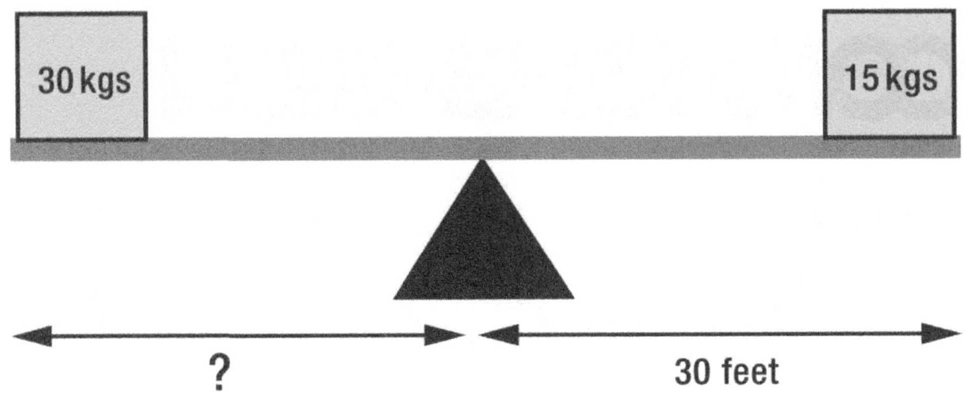

A. 5 feet

B. 10 feet.

C. 15 feet.

D. 45 feet.

QUESTION 4

A block and tackle refers to a device which is used to:

A. Place under the wheel of a car to stop it from rolling backwards.

B. Catch large fish.

C. Leverage a stationary object.

D. Hoist an object upwards by means of rope and pulleys.

QUESTION 5

In the diagram, the spring can be stretched 1 inch by a force of 200 pounds. How much force needs to be applied to the object in order to move the object 4.5 inches to the left?

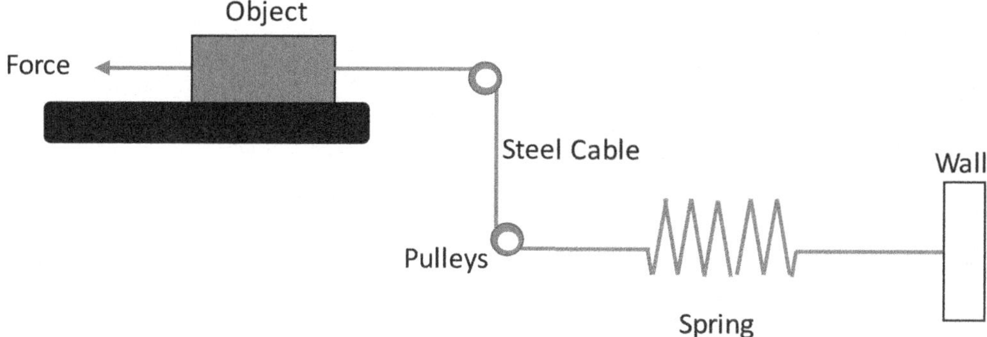

A. 900 lbs.

B. 450 lbs.

C. 800 lbs.

D. 90 lbs.

QUESTION 6

Which of the following scenarios requires overcoming the least amount of kinetic force?

A. Pushing an empty washing machine box down a path.

B. Pushing a washing machine in its box down a path.

C. Pushing an empty washing machine box down an icy path.

D. Pushing a washing machine in its box down an icy path.

QUESTION 7

If a ramp is 12 feet long and 3 feet high, how much effort is required to move a 200-pound object up the ramp?

A. 600 lbs.

B. 50 bs.

C. 200 lbs.

D. 150 lbs.

QUESTION 8

If cog A turns anticlockwise at a speed of 20 rpm (revolutions per minute), how will cog B turn?

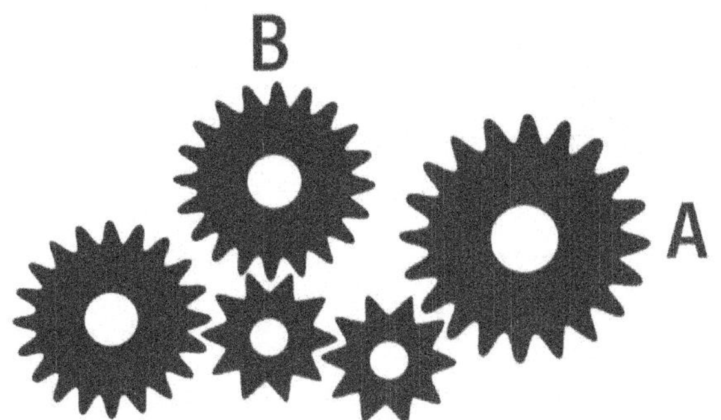

A. Clockwise, 20 rpm

B. Anti-clockwise, 20 rpm

C. Clockwise, 10 rpm

D. Anti-clockwise, 10 rpm

QUESTION 9

The use of an earth-fault loop test is to make sure that...

A. Enough current is passable to open the protective device.

B. No charge can pass through.

C. The voltage through the circuit remains low.

D. The earth wire is connected safely and correctly.

QUESTION 10

In order to lift the 3,000-pound weight, approximately how many pounds would you need to pull down with?

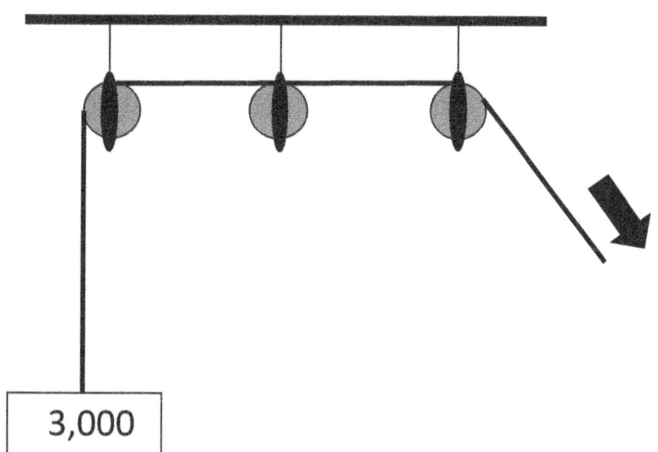

A. 1,000 lbs

B. 500 lbs.

C. 3,000 lbs.

D. 50 lbs.

ANSWERS TO AUTO AND SHOP INFORMATION PRACTICE QUESTIONS

Q1. C. Dam

Q2. D. Frictional Force

Q3. C. 15 feet

Q4. D. Hoist an object upwards by means of rope and pulleys

Q5. A. 900 lbs

Q6. C. Pushing an empty washing machine box down an icy path

Q7. B. 50 lbs

Q8. A. Clockwise, 20 rpm

Q9. A. Enough current is passable to open the protective device.

Q10. C. 3,000 lbs

Now move on to the Assembling Objects subtest of the ASVAB.

ASSEMBLING OBJECTS

The Assembling Objects section of the ASVAB requires you to have strong visual spatial ability.

During this section of your Armed Forces assessment, the number of questions and the duration you have will depend on whether you are sitting the paper-based or computer-based version.

Subtest	Computer version	Paper version	Content
Assembling Objects (AO)	16 questions 15 minutes	25 questions 15 minutes	Spatial Orientation

PLEASE NOTE: the Assembling Objects (AO) section has **NO** impact on your Armed Forces Qualification Test (AFQT) score. However, don't take this as an opportunity to relax.

The score for this subtest will be used to calculate military composite scores for job qualification basis.

Use this chapter as a mini lesson to improve your spatial ability. Below we have outlined the key areas that you should be focusing on:

SPATIAL AWARENESS	VIZUALIZATION	INTERPRETATION	COGNITIVE SKILLS

<u>This subtest will comprise of two types of Assembing Objects question:</u>

- **CONNECTION PROBLEMS** – you will be required to mentally attach lines and shapes together.

- **PUZZLE PROBLEMS** – you will be required to take shapes and mentally connect them to create a new shape.

In this type of question, you will be presented with five drawings. The first drawing will include various disassembled parts. The other four drawings will show these parts connected. Your task is to work out which of the drawings show the parts connected correctly.

<u>Below is an example of how the questions will be presented:</u>

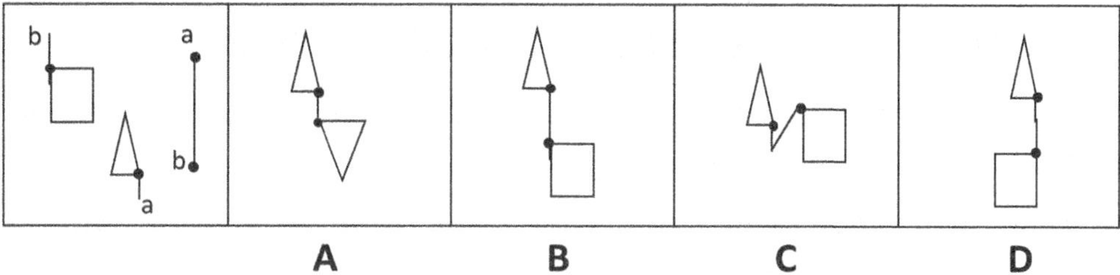

In the example, the correct answer is option B. Choice A includes shapes that are not in the original drawing. Although Choices C and D have the correct shapes, they are not connected at the same points as shown in the original drawing.

For these types of questions, the shapes may be rotated or reoriented from the first drawing.

Below we have outlined some crucial advice that you MUST remember when answering these questions:

THE DIFFERENCE BETWEEN REFLECTIONS AND ROTATIONS

It is important that you remember the difference between reflections and rotations. Reflecting, also known as mirroring and flipping, means that no matter what way you rotate the shape, it will never look like the original shape.

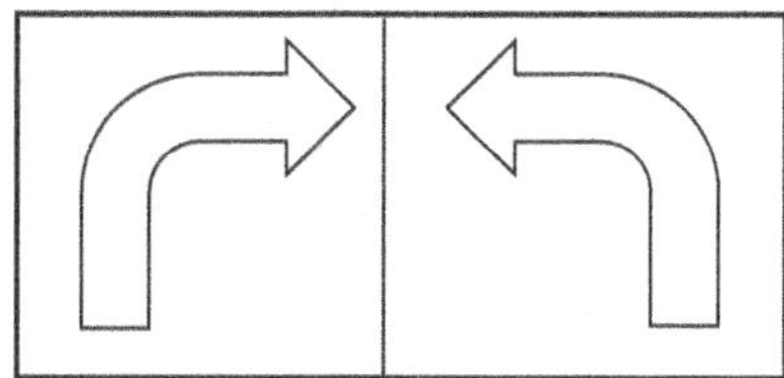

As you see in the above diagram, no matter what way you rotate the first shape, it will never look like the second. This is because it has been reflected.

The reason we have included some information on this is because the Assembling Objects subtest is designed to catch you out. Simple things like spotting mirroring is crucial to obtaining top marks.

USING THE CORRECT PLACES TO CROSS OVER

You need to pay attention to where the lines are drawn in order to connect the two shapes.

If a line starts in the centre of a shape, you need to ensure that the answer you choose also contains a line starting in the same place.

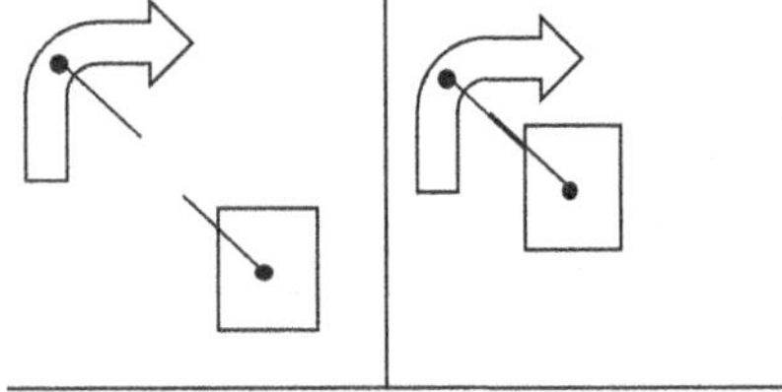

As you can see in the above example, the points in both shapes begin in the centre of the shape. Therefore, your answer should replicate the same positioning as shown in the first drawing.

Puzzle Problem Questions

This type of question is often found easier than the first. This is because the question requires you to connect shapes together, just like a jigsaw puzzle.

The only thing you may struggle with in regards to this type of question is visualizing the shapes to twist and rotate them in order to fit with other shape pieces.

<u>Below is an example of how the questions will be presented:</u>

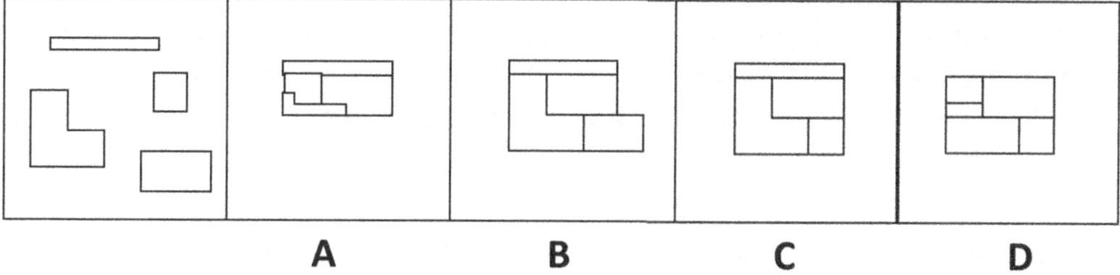

In the example, the correct answer is C. By mentally sliding the four shapes together, the end result would look like answer option C. Choices A, B and D can be ruled out because one or more shapes have been manipulated in some way. For example, in choice D, the thin, long rectangle has been shortened.

For these types of questions, the shapes may be rotated or reoriented from the first drawing.

ASSEMBLING OBJECTS

QUICK TIPS

- The definition of spatial reasoning is 'The ability to interpret and make drawings from mental images and visualise movement or change in those images.' The sample test questions within this guide will help you to improve in the areas of visualising and interpreting movement in shapes and diagrams.

- The more practice you undergo, the better your scores will be. The only way to improve spatial reasoning is to attempt questions and understand the logic and reasoning of each of them.

- If you don't know the answer, take an educated guess. You can eliminate some of the options you know to be incorrect.

- Keep an eye on the time. Remember you only have 15 minutes to answer all 25 questions for the paper-version of the ASVAB (15 minutes to answer 16 questions on the computer-version). That works out to be around 36 seconds per question!

- As with any test, it is important to undergo in-depth revision. The only way to enhance your knowledge is to improve your mental awareness and spatial reasoning skills. Break up your revision time using a timetable. Focus on the areas that you are not so confident with.

ASSEMBLING OBJECTS

PRACTICE QUESTIONS

QUESTION 1

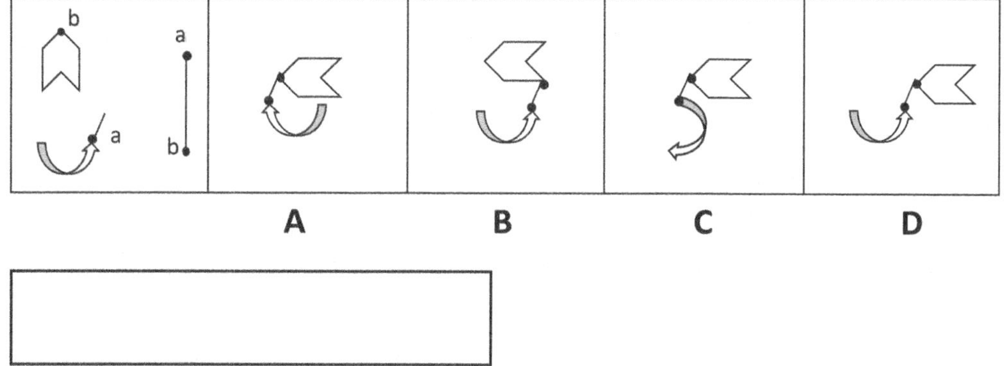

A　　**B**　　**C**　　**D**

QUESTION 2

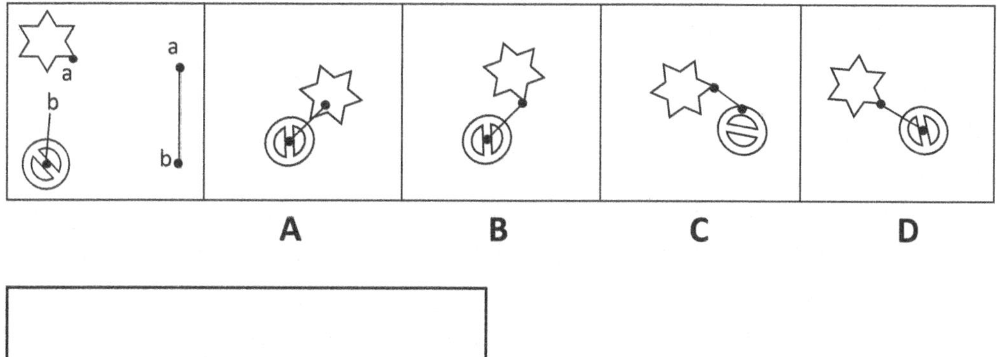

A　　**B**　　**C**　　**D**

QUESTION 3

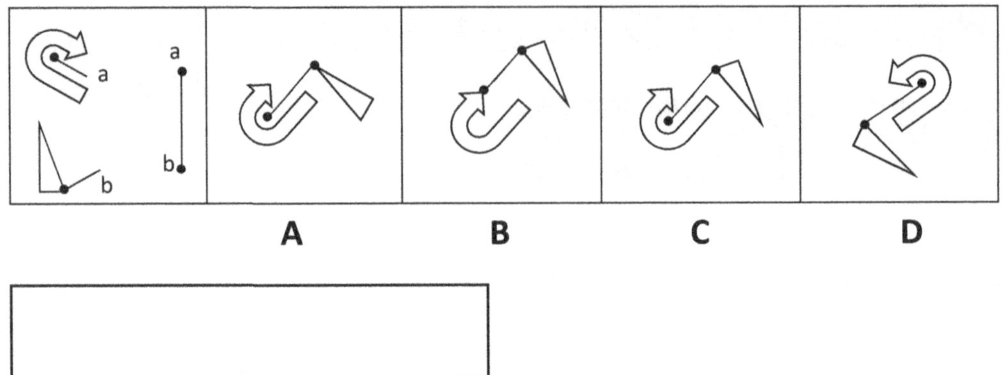

QUESTION 4

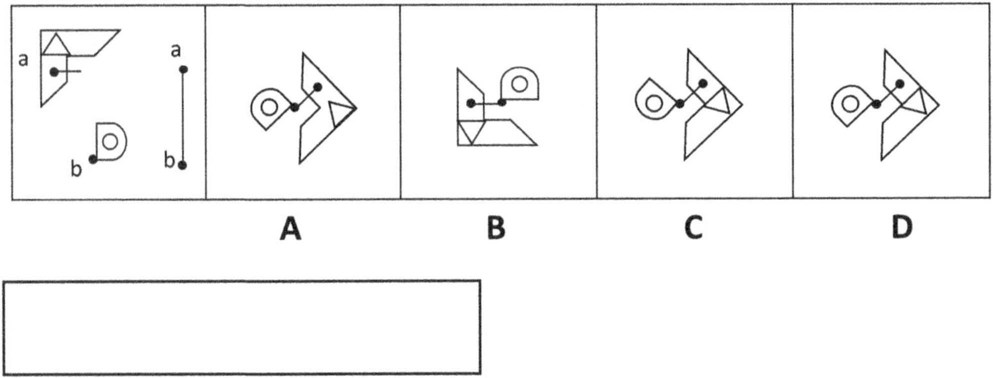

QUESTION 5

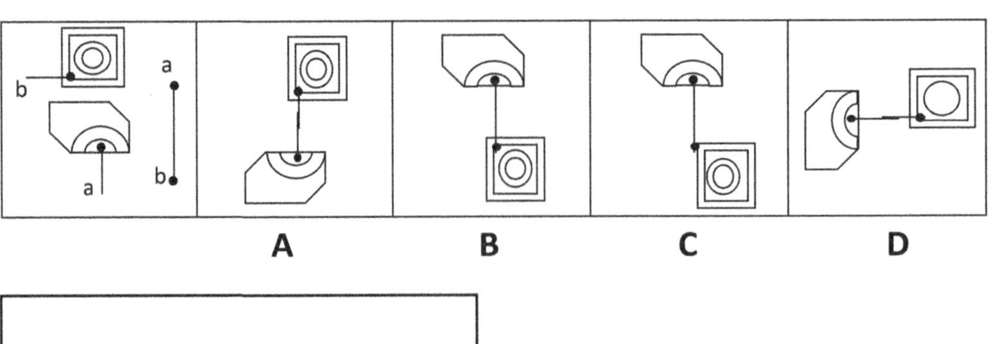

QUESTION 6

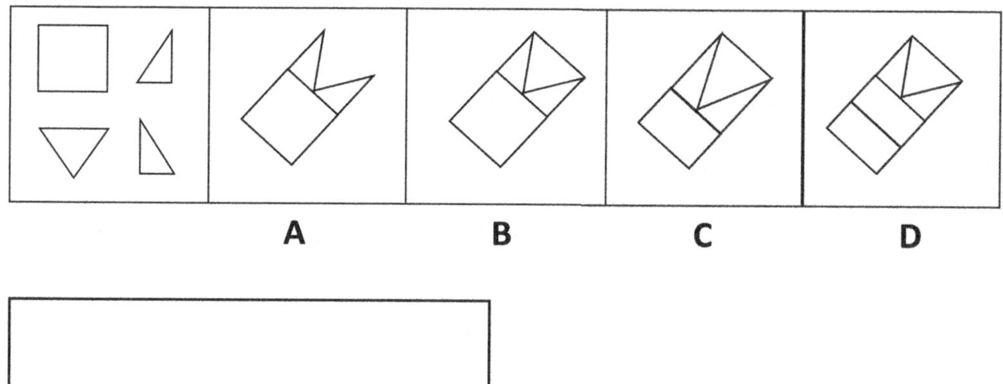

QUESTION 7

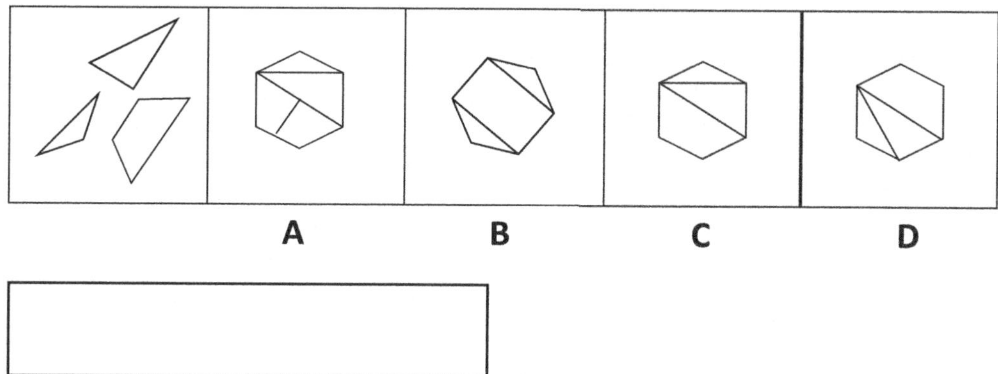

QUESTION 8

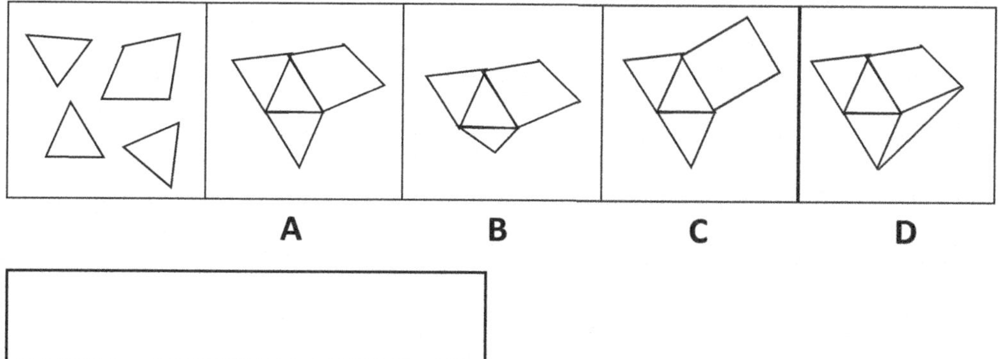

QUESTION 9

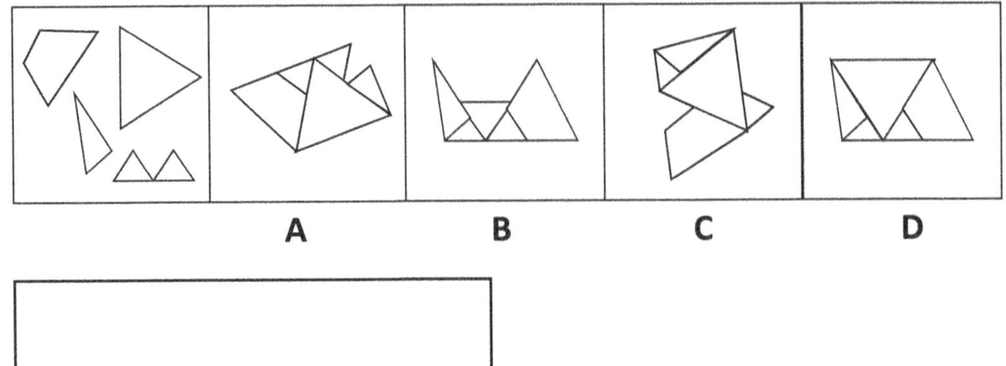

QUESTION 10

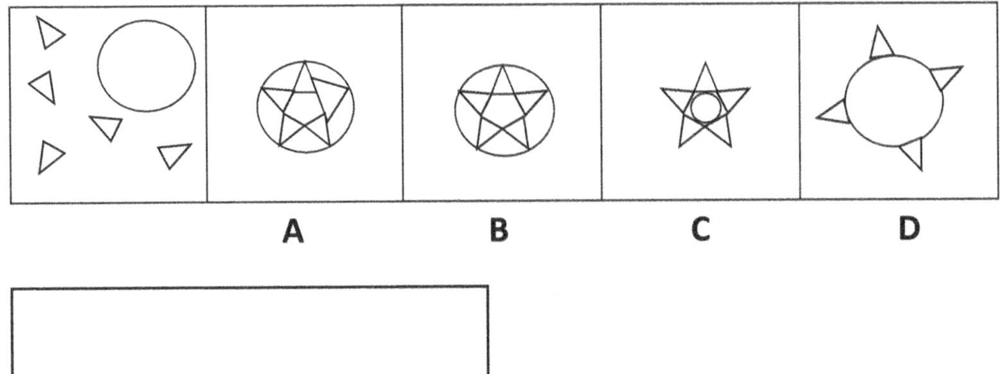

ANSWERS TO ASSEMBLING OBJECTS PRACTICE QUESTIONS

Q1. D

Q2. B

Q3. C

Q4. D

Q5. B

Q6. B

Q7. C

Q8. A

Q9. D

Q10. B

You have now completed all subsections of the ASVAB.

ASVAB PRACTICE TEST

How2Become

Armed Services Vocational Aptitude Battery

ASVAB

Practice Tests for the United States Military

2 hours and 30 minutes

Materials

- This is a practice test based on the paper-version of the ASVAB.

Instructions

- There are **9** subtests in total.

- You need to answer **all** of the questions.

- Use a **black** pen.

© HOW2BECOME.COM

The test will be formatted in the order shown here. We have provided you with a quick overview of how many questions there are, the time limit, and a brief description of each subtest.

Subtest	Paper version	Content
General Science (GS)	25 questions 11 minutes	General biological and physical principles
Arithmetic Reasoning (AR)	30 questions 36 minutes	Word problems requiring high school knowledge
Word Knowledge (WK)	35 questions 11 minutes	Correct word meaning
Paragraph Comprehension (PC)	15 questions 13 minutes	Read a passage and answer questions
Mathematics Knowledge (MK)	25 questions 24 minutes	High school mathematical knowledge
Electronics Information (EI)	20 questions 9 minutes	General electronic principles
Auto & Shop Information (AS)	25 questions 11 minutes	Knowledge of tools and automobiles
Mechanical Comprehension (MC)	25 questions 19 minutes	Basic mechanical knowledge
Assembling Objects (AO)	25 questions 15 minutes	Spatial orientation

General Science

You have **11** minutes to complete **25** questions.

QUESTION 1

The female part of a flower is called...

A. Stamen.

B. Pistil.

C. Anther.

D. Sepal.

QUESTION 2

What is it called when an object tries to resist the change in motion?

A. Law of Friction.

B. Law of Order.

C. Law of Inertia.

D. Law of Momentum.

QUESTION 3

Which of the atmospheric layers contains the ozone layer?

A. Stratosphere.

B. Thermosphere.

C. Troposphere.

D. Mesosphere.

QUESTION 4

Which planet in the solar system is the coldest?

A. Mars.

B. Mercury.

C. Neptune.

D. Saturn.

QUESTION 5

What is the role of metabolism in the human body?

A. Chemical processes in the body which allow growth, production of energy and elimination of waste materials.

B. The process of digesting food which is absorbed by the body.

C. Catalyst substances that increase the rate of chemical reactions within the body.

D. All of the above.

QUESTION 6

The ability to influence an organism's genotype is often referred to as...

A. Natual selection.

B. Hybrids.

C. Common selection.

D. Artificial selection.

QUESTION 7

Which planet in the solar system is the hottest?

A. Earth

B. Venus.

C. Neptune.

D. Saturn.

QUESTION 8

Which solid is formed when copper carbonate is heated?

A. Copper sulfide.

B. Copper nitrate.

C. Copper.

D. Copper oxide.

QUESTION 9

A panel of solar cells has an efficiency of 0.35. The total power input to the panel is 4.6 kW. Work out the useful power output of this panel of social cells in kW.

A. 4.25 kW.

B. 1.61 kW.

C. 0.82 kW.

D. None of the above.

QUESTION 10

Which of the following is the name for the colored, flat, ring-shaped membrane of the eye?

A. Iris.

B. Pupil.

C. Cornea.

D. Lens.

QUESTION 11

How long does it take for Earth to rotate 90 degrees?

A. 12 hours.

B. 24 hours.

C. 1 year.

D. 6 hours.

QUESTION 12

In the presence of a catalyst, ethanol is produced from ethene by hydration. Which of the following best defines hydration?

A. Reaction with pollution.

B. Mixing with water.

C. Reaction with steam or water.

D. All of the above.

QUESTION 13

Which of the following scientific disciplines best defines the study of insects and bugs?

A. Paleontology.

B. Geology.

C. Ecology.

D. Entomology.

QUESTION 14

If the temperature in Fahrenheit is 140°, the temperature in Celsius is...

A. 100°

B. 80°

C. 120°

D. 60°

QUESTION 15

Which of the following is the Earth's air mostly composed of?

A. Oxygen.

B. Hydrogen.

C. Nitrogen.

D. Carbon Dioxide.

QUESTION 16

Coal is a fossil fuel. It consists of hydrogen, carbon, oxygen and what other element?

A. Sulfur.

B. Potassium.

C. Mineral water.

D. Petroleum.

QUESTION 17

Which gas does not condense when the remaining gases are cooled to -200°C?

A. Oxygen.

B. Argon.

C. Neon.

D. Carbon dioxide.

QUESTION 18

Which of the following best describes why wind turbines operate at maximum power output for only 30% of the time?

A. When wind reaches a certain speed, the turbine reduces its power.

B. Wind is unreliable and varies.

C. If the temperature gets too hot, the wind turbine will reduce its power.

D. None of the above.

QUESTION 19

How long does it take Earth to complete an orbit of the Sun?

A. 1 year.

B. 6 months.

C. 24 hours.

D. 42 hours.

QUESTION 20

Which of the following best describes the cause of the aurora borealis?

A. Collisions between electrically uncharged particles are released from the Sun and collide with oxygen and nitrogen.

B. The Earth, sun and moon align, which causes a change in the Earth's atmospheric gases.

C. Collisions between electrically charged particles are released from the Sun and collide with oxygen and nitrogen.

D. Positive and negative charges grow large enough and cause electrical charges within the Earth's atmosphere.

QUESTION 21

Oxygenated blood enters the heart through which of the following?

A. Left atrium.

B. Right ventricle.

C. Right atrium.

D. Left ventricle.

QUESTION 22

The instrument to measure atmospheric pressue is...

A. Anemometer.

B. Thermometer.

C. Sphygmomanometer.

D. Barometer.

QUESTION 23

What is a pathogen?

A. A germ, bacterium or virus that can cause diseases.

B. The growth and development of female reproductive system.

C. A steroid hormone used to prevent ovulation.

D. None of the above.

QUESTION 24

The terrestrial planets in The Solar System are...

A. Earth.

B. Venus, Jupiter, Saturn and Uranus.

C. Mercury, Venus, Earth and Mars.

D. Any planet.

QUESTION 25

How is a nerve impulse transmitted through the nervous system?

A. An influx of calcium chloride ions.

B. Break down of blood cells which react to human senses.

C. Electric potential.

D. A combination of all three.

Arithmetic Reasoning

You have **36** minutes to complete **30** questions.

QUESTION 1

Simplify the following:

$$6\tfrac{3}{8} + 2\tfrac{1}{5} - 3\tfrac{2}{7}$$

A. $8\tfrac{81}{140}$

B. $5\tfrac{2}{15}$

C. $5\tfrac{81}{280}$

D. $8\tfrac{60}{120}$

QUESTION 2

How many imperial pints are in 63 imperial gallons?

A. 504 pints.

B. 128 pints.

C. 300 pints.

D. 10 pints.

QUESTION 3

Which of the following is not an equivalent fraction to $\frac{1}{3}$?

A. $\frac{2}{6}$

B. $\frac{13}{39}$

C. $\frac{3}{6}$

D. $\frac{27}{81}$

QUESTION 4

An English class of 28 have just sat a mock exam. The exam has 2 sections – Literature and Language. It takes approximately 6 minutes to mark the Literature section and 7 minutes to mark the Language section. Another 2 minutes is given on each exam to check the work again. How long in hours and minutes does it take to mark the English mock exam?

A. 6 hours and 45 minutes.

B. 5 hours and 25 minutes.

C. 7 hours.

D. 9 hours and 10 minutes.

QUESTION 5

How many grams are there in 2.5 kilograms?

A. 0.0025g

B. 250g

C. 2,005g

D. 2,500g

QUESTION 6

Which answer is equivalent to eight to the fifth power?

A. 32,768

B. 1

C. 0

D. 40

QUESTION 7

What is 95,000,000,000 in scientific notation?

A. 95×10^{10}

B. 9.5×10^{-10}

C. 0.9×10^{11}

D. 9.5×10^{10}

QUESTION 8

Petunia is getting married and needs to be ready to leave at 11:25am. If the current time is 7:05am, how long does she have before she needs to leave?

A. $4 \frac{1}{2}$ hours.

B. $4 \frac{1}{3}$ hours.

C. $5 \frac{1}{2}$ hours.

D. $4 \frac{2}{3}$ hours.

QUESTION 9

What is one quarter of 6 hours?

A. 1 hour and 30 minutes.

B. 95 minutes.

C. 180 minutes.

D. 1 hour and 20 minutes.

QUESTION 10

A farmer has 630 eggs. They are to be placed in egg trays. Each tray can hold 36 eggs. How many trays will be needed to hold all of the eggs?

A. 17

B. 16

C. 18

D. 20

QUESTION 11

A flight leaves the airport at 2200 hours. It is an 11 hour and 45 minute flight. There is a 2 hour time difference. What time will they arrive at their destination, assuming the time difference is 2 hours in front?

A. 12 noon.

B. 11:45am

C. 9:45am.

D. 13:00.

QUESTION 12

You are going to drive to your friend's house. She lives 17 miles away from you with an average speed limit of 30mph. Your friend asks for an estimated time of arrival. If you leave your house at 1415, and you stick to the speed limit, what time will you arrive at your friend's house? (Assuming there is no traffic).

A. 14:49

B. 15:00

C. 14:32

D. 15:04

QUESTION 13

A lady has been prescribed medication by her doctor. She is prescribed a 10.5 fluid ounce bottle of medication with the instructions to take 0.25 fluid ounces three times a day. How many days does she have to take the medication for?

A. 7 days.

B. 14 days.

C. 21 days.

D. 10 days.

QUESTION 14

A farmland is measured to be 220m in length by 80m in width. What is the approximate area of the field in hectares? 1 hectare = 10,000m^2 = 2.47 acres.

A. 17 hectares

B. 1.76 hectares

C. 176 hectares.

D. 7.67 hectares.

QUESTION 15

The sterling to US dollar rate is 1:1.32. How many dollars would you receive if you changed up £450?

A. $592

B. $541

C. $594

D. $441

QUESTION 16

Martha went to a beauty salon. She spent $42.60 for a wash, cut and blow dry, $15.95 on a manicure, and $27.50 on a 30-minute neck massage. How much did Martha spend in total?

A. $65.05

B. $68.05

C. $86.05

D. $86.50

QUESTION 17

What is the price of a $2,500 item after successive discounts of 15% and 25%?

A. $1,593.75

B. $2,125.25

C. $1,593

D. $2,125

QUESTION 18

What is the area of a room measured 50 feet wide and 52 feet long?

A. 2,200ft^2

B. 1,600ft^2

C. 60ft^2

D. 2,600ft^2

QUESTION 19

Sally wants to buy a car for a price of $45,000. She takes out a 4 year loan with a compound interest rate of 7.2%. How much will Sally have to pay for the car with the added interest? To the nearest whole number.

A. $50,000

B. $56,000

C. $59,428

D. $59,690

QUESTION 20

If you type 52 word per minute, how many words can you type in 20 minutes?

A. 1,000

B. 1,020

C. 1,040

D. 1,400

QUESTION 21

Thirteen plus fifty-six is divided by a number. If the result is 3, what's the number?

A. 23

B. 20

C. 6

D. 12

QUESTION 22

A square has an area of 441cm^2. What is the perimeter?

A. 221 cm

B. 21 cm

C. 30 cm

D. 55 cm

QUESTION 23

A map of Atlanta has a scale of 1 cm = 16 km. The actual distance between Atlanta and Tallahassee is about 368 kilometers. How far apart are the cities on the map?

A. 18 cm.

B. 45 cm.

C. 36 cm.

D. 23 cm.

QUESTION 24

Three whole numbers add up to a total of 100. The first number is a multiple of 15. The second number is ten times the third number. Both the second and the third number are a multiple of 5. Work out the three numbers.

A. 35, 55 and 5.

B. 20, 50 and 5.

C. 45, 50 and 5.

D. None of the above.

QUESTION 25

Add $^7/_9$ of 189 to $^5/_8$ of 128.

A. 221

B. 227

C. 235

D. 237

QUESTION 26

What is the sum of the integers from 1 to 200?

A. 18,300

B. 20,000

C. 20,000

D. 20,100

QUESTION 27

Tammy has been walking at a constant pace of 2.5 miles per hour. She has been walking for 36 minutes. How many miles has she walked?

A. 0.5 miles

B. 5.5 miles.

C. 1.5 miles.

D. 3 miles.

QUESTION 28

Tabitha's general knowledge quiz scores are 38, 42, 27 and 59. Each quiz is marked out of 60. What is Tabitha's average score?

A. 41.5

B. 45

C. 38

D. 45.5

QUESTION 29

A field is shown on a map. The field measures 6cm by 8cm on the map and the scale of the map is 1 : 6,000. Given that 10,000m^2 is equivalent to 1 hectare, what is the area of the field in real life in hectares?

A. 16 hectares

B. 28.8 hectares

C. 19 hectares

D. 20.55 hectares

QUESTION 30

A sequence uses the following rule: n^{th} term = 3(n + 1). Work out the 30th term in the sequence.

A. 31

B. 103.

C. 93

D. 97.

Word Knowledge

You have **11** minutes to complete **35** questions.

QUESTION 1

The word most opposite in meaning to <u>imaginary</u> is...

A. Actual.

B. Legendary.

C. Non-Existent.

D. Pretend.

QUESTION 2

<u>Abundance</u> most nearly means..

A. Unique.

B. Abysmal.

C. Catastrophic.

D. Plethora.

QUESTION 3

Which word does not have a similar meaning to <u>talkative</u>?

A. Garrulous.

B. Loquacious.

C. Affluent.

D. Voluble.

QUESTION 4

Simon <u>admonished</u> his sister about coming into his room.

A. Complimented.

B. Encouraged.

C. Threatened.

D. Ignored.

QUESTION 5

Which word does not have a similar meaning to <u>result</u>?

A. Outcome.

B. Effect.

C. Upshot.

D. Affect.

QUESTION 6

The word most opposite in meaning to <u>stimulate</u> is...

A. Hook.

B. Rouse.

C. Prod.

D. Dissuade.

QUESTION 7

Peter became quite <u>melancholic</u> when he reflected on his life.

A. Intriqued.

B. Unimpressed.

C. Optimistic.

D. Saddened.

QUESTION 8

<u>Desensitize</u> mostly means...

A. Active.

B. Engaged.

C. Improper.

D. Nonreactive.

QUESTION 9

The decision didn't <u>augur</u> well.

A. Recount.

B. Warrant.

C. Bode.

D. Receive.

QUESTION 10

Johnny <u>spendthrift</u> his inheritance in less than 6 months.

A. Saved.

B. Wasted.

C. Obtained.

D. Probed.

QUESTION 11

<u>Indolent</u> mostly means...

A. Rudeness.

B. Lethargic.

C. Contempt.

D. Offended.

QUESTION 12

He will be <u>extradited</u> to Japan from England.

A. Deported.

B. Fibrous.

C. Connected.

D. Sold.

QUESTION 13

<u>Convalesce</u> mostly means...

A. Relapsed.

B. Removal.

C. Recuperate.

D. Retribute.

QUESTION 14

Which word does not have a similar meaning to <u>abnegation</u>?

A. Self-denial.

B. Rejection.

C. Abstinence.

D. Sanction.

QUESTION 15

She was treated like a <u>pariah</u> in her own community.

A. Ghost.

B. Player.

C. Royal.

D. Outsider.

QUESTION 16

Which of the following does not have a similar meaning to <u>pellucid</u>?

A. Luminous.

B. Unclear.

C. Crystalling.

D. Explicit.

QUESTION 17

<u>Sanguine</u> mostly means...

A. Sallow.

B. Shifty.

C. Rapacity.

D. Buoyant.

QUESTION 18

<u>Ubiquitous</u> mostly means...

A. Omnipresent.

B. Tactful.

C. Demeaning.

D. Meagre.

QUESTION 19

Which of the following does not have a similar meaning to <u>umbrage</u>?

A. Nettling.

B. Exasperation.

C. Gleeful.

D. Grudge.

QUESTION 20

Tom wrote a speech to <u>vilify</u> his opponent.

A. Teach.

B. Shake.

C. Torment.

D. Slander.

QUESTION 21

Her ideas brought up a huge <u>tirade</u> about global warming and climate change.

A. Tantrum.

B. Persona.

C. Rant.

D. Atmosphere.

QUESTION 22

<u>Vitriolic</u> mostly means...

A. Troublesome.

B. Scathing.

C. Mindful.

D. Lavished.

QUESTION 23

Which word is most opposite in meaning to <u>solipsism</u>?

A. Objectivity.

B. Martyrdom.

C. Subjectivity.

D. Empathy.

QUESTION 24

Which of the following does not have a similar meaning to <u>flagrant</u>?

A. Meek.

B. Conspicuous.

C. Arrant.

D. Egregious.

QUESTION 25

<u>Embezzlement</u> mostly means...

A. Bewilderment.

B. Compensation.

C. Captivating.

D. Larceny.

QUESTION 26

The mental <u>duress</u> caused the suspect to cry.

A. Release.

B. Indearment.

C. Health.

D. Pressure.

QUESTION 27

Which of the following does not have a similar meaning to <u>arcane</u>?

A. Impenetrable.

B. Unknowable.

C. Mystic.

D. Outward.

QUESTION 28

David lived in a <u>sumptuous</u> building.

A. Small.

B. Plain.

C. Luxuriant.

D. Derelict.

QUESTION 29

The moonlight will <u>adumbrate</u> an eerie silhouette of the wolf.

A. Sketch.

B. Release.

C. Illuminate.

D. Spook.

QUESTION 30

Which of the following does not have a similar meaning to <u>abject</u>?

A. Commendable.

B. Degraded.

C. Worthless.

D. Pitiable.

QUESTION 31

<u>Dogmatic</u> mostly means...

A. Vicious.

B. Atrocious.

C. Domineering.

D. Dubious.

QUESTION 32

<u>Ebullient</u> mostly means...

A. Disinterested.

B. Irrepressible.

C. Intuitive.

D. Radical.

QUESTION 33

Which of the following does not have a similar meaning to <u>grandiloquent</u>?

A. Unpretentious.

B. Fustian.

C. Pompous.

D. Inflated.

QUESTION 34

Vinnie's <u>impetuous</u> behavour landed him in a prison cell.

A. Thought-provoking.

B. Cautious.

C. Ardent.

D. Frigid.

QUESTION 35

Tommie's drinking has started to <u>impinge</u> upon his family.

A. Dodge.

B. Affect.

C. Rely.

D. Undermine.

Paragraph Comprehension

You have **13** minutes to complete **15** questions.

The popularity of modern football has reached an all-time high. Football is by far and away the most popular sport in the world. In a way, you could argue football has transcended sport itself. It has become a language, a means to bridge the gap between different kinds of people.

Unfortunately, as its popularity grows, so does the desperation to win. Now more than ever, the financial rewards for winning in football have grown disproportionate, and this has given rise to a new form of sporting cancer – diving.

Diving (or flopping as it's known in the USA) is the practice of faking or exaggerating injury, in order to con or cheat the referee – thereby gaining an advantage. Whether that advantage is a free kick or a penalty, the result is irrelevant. The bottom line is that this has to stop. The phrase 'football is a man's game' is horrendously outdated, but there is some truth behind it. Not only is diving cheating, but it slows the game down. It's embarrassing to watch perfectly healthy athletes pretending to be hurt, and it's even worse when your team suffers the consequences of it. Cheating is cheating, plain and simple. We need to kick this out of the game, before it kills football altogether.

QUESTION 1

What is the overall point that the author is trying to make?

A. Diving is not manly.

B. Diving is embarrassing.

C. Diving is outdated.

D. Diving needs to be stopped.

QUESTION 2

In paragraph 2, the author uses the term 'bottom line'. What is the name for this type of phrase?

A. Idiomatic.

B. Platonic.

C. Idiosyncratic.

D. Nomothetic.

One hundred and fifty students from a high school voluntarily attended a protest in aid to show their views on animal testing. At the protest, the main view displayed was that animal testing was "inhumane, unfair and morally wrong". This topic was selected as one of the most problematic amongst the Environmental Science students. They showed a strong belief against animal testing and displayed a sense of moral obligation to defend animals from animal cruelty.

QUESTION 3

According to this passage,

A. The students showed little interest in animal welfare.

B. High schools place huge emphasis on animal cruetly.

C. The students showed clear passion about animal rights.

D. All of the above.

QUESTION 4

Which of the following statements is not supported by the above passage?

A. One of the views of animal testing is that it's morally unacceptable.

B. Environmental students were heavily concerned with animal welfare.

C. The students played an active role in putting their views across in a civilized protest.

D. The Environmental Science students were currently studying animal testing.

The case of a Mumbai couple who approached the courts in India after their time limit for an abortion was overdue and wanted a termination of their pregnancy. This case of euthanasia was denied by the courts. The parents wanted to be granted permission for an abortion, after they found out that the foetus had been detected to have disabilities which would affect the life of the unborn child. The courts argued that the unborn child has the right to live despite being possibly disabled.

QUESTION 5

Which of the following statements is untrue based on the passage?

A. The courts stated that unborn children still have a right to life despite any disabilities.

B. The courts of Mumbai believe that the child has no rights because it is unborn.

C. There is a time limit for sanctioning abortions.

D. Mumbai's laws allow for termination of pregnancies.

QUESTION 6

What is not spoken about in this passage?

A. Pregnancy.

B. Adoption.

C. Court cases.

D. Mumbai's laws allow for termination of pregnancies.

Child labour has always been a significant global issue associated with poverty, inadequate education, lack of opportunity and a range of health issues. Developing continents such as Africa, Asia and Latin America are among the biggest countries in which child labour is at its highest. Such working conditions jeopardize children's health and lifestyles. They are made to work at a very young age, are malnourished and work long hours in unpleasant working conditions.

QUESTION 7

Which of the following statements can you assume from this passage?

A. Poverty is at its highest.

B. Africa, Asia and Latin America are the biggest continents which suffer the biggest health problems.

C. Work is available for all ages in all continents.

D. Child labour is more apparent in poverty-stricken continents.

> Children are at a vulnerable age where influences and role models are crucial. Children spend large parts of their days at school and have become somewhat influenced by their teachers.

QUESTION 8

Which of the following assumptions can be made from this passage?

A. Children are at the age where their minds are engaging with the world around them, meaning they are viable to change at anytime.

B. Children have great intelligence and therefore are able to make up their own minds about what is wrong and what is right.

C. Teachers are the only example of role models for children.

D. Because of a child's age and their naïve manner, they are easily influenced and thus will act in the same way they are shown.

QUESTION 9

What is being described in this passage?

A. Cognitive ability.

B. Social intervention.

C. Child development.

D. Mental health.

Children between the ages of 8 months and 6 years old were studied in regards to their language. The study indicates that children are at their most significant developing stages. Research claims that children who learn more than 1 language or sign language from an early age have better brain development. Multilingualism is quite often proven to enhance your child's education and develop better reading and writing skills.

QUESTION 10

Which of the following is inferred from this passage?

A. Learning multiple languages from an early age helps children's social skills.

B. Learning multiple languages from an early age helps children's brain development.

C. Learning multiple languages reduces children's intelligence.

D. Education and writing skills for children are at an all time low.

QUESTION 11

In the passage above, multilingualism is defined as...

A. The use of one language.

B. The inability to use the correct language.

C. The use of more than one language.

D. The inability to speak your native language.

Fathers-to-be have the right to at least two weeks paid paternity leave. The Government have also introduced an Additional Paternity Leave whereby the parents are able to take six months off work, and receive the maternity pay that the mother would have got if she continued her maternity leave. This way both parents are able to enjoy the first 6 months off with their new-born.

QUESTION 12

Which of the following assumptions can be made from this passage?

A. Before the scheme for Additional Paternity Leave was introduced, fathers were unable to take paternity leave.

B. Fathers are entitled to at least two weeks of paternity leave and possibly more depending on circumstances and their employers.

C. Fathers are entitled to the same amount of leave as mothers.

D. Paternity leave is weighed up based on each individual case.

A physician tells a patient that eating a plum a day helps control heart rate and blood pressure. Plums have plenty of minerals like potassium and iron, which are essential components for a healthy body.

QUESTION 13

Which of the following assumptions is not made based on this passage?

A. Your blood pressure will increase after eating a plum.

B. It can be assumed that the patient either has a problem with her heart rate or her blood pressure.

C. Potassium and iron can be found to control heart rate and blood pressure.

D. Your blood pressure will decrease after eating a plum.

A bank got robbed in the early hours of Saturday morning. There were 8 hostages, 3 of them being employees at the bank. A man in a balaclava pointed a gun at one of the bankers and demanded the money from her till. She handed the money to the man in the balaclava at the same time he was tackled from behind by one of the hostages. A gunshot went off.

QUESTION 14

Based on this passage...

A. You can conclude that this was a planned robbery.

B. The person who tackled the man in the balaclava was a man.

C. You can conclude that the robber was arrested.

D. You cannot infer if anyone was shot.

QUESTION 15

It is reasonable to believe, based on this passage, that 5 of the hostages were...

A. Bankers.

B. Robbers.

C. Customers.

D. Police officers.

Mathematics Knowledge

You have **24** minutes to complete **25** questions.

QUESTION 1

Work out $\dfrac{4}{6} \times \dfrac{3}{5}$

A. $^2/_5$

B. $^1/_5$

C. $^3/_4$

D. $^1/_4$

QUESTION 2

The following table shows the percentage of nickel in two UK coins.

COIN	WEIGHT	NICKEL
50p coin	8g	25%
20p coin	5g	16%

If both the coins are made of only nickel and copper, what is the difference between the weight of copper present in the 50 pence coin and the weight of copper in the 20 pence coin?

A. 1.3g

B. 2.5g

C. 1.8g

D. 2g

QUESTION 3

Factorize completely:

$$20a^2 - 10a$$

A. 10a (2a – 1)

B. 5a (2a – 1)

C. 10a (2a + 1)

D. 5a (2a + 1)

QUESTION 4

Solve the following linear inequality:

$$2 - 6x \leq -8x - 4$$

A. x ≤ -3

B. x > -3

C. x ≥ -3

D. x < -3

QUESTION 5

Work out the value of x.

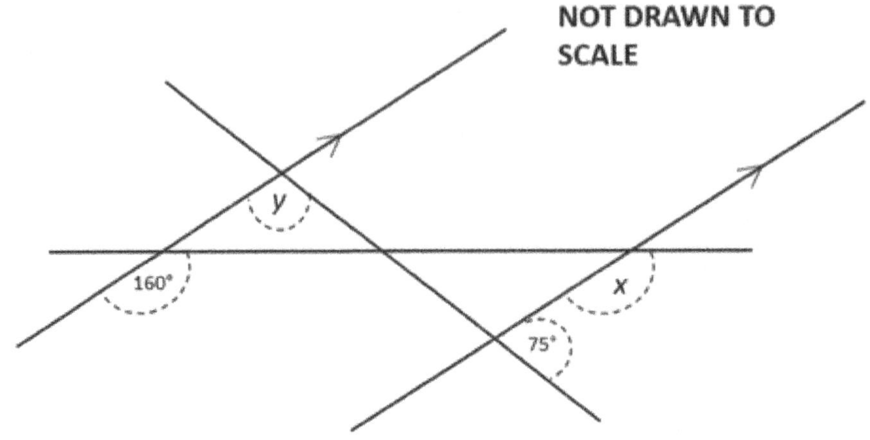

A. 75°

B. 100°

C. 160°

D. 125°

QUESTION 6

One of the short sides of a triangle measures 5cm. The other short side measures 8cm. Work out the length of the hypotenuse.

A. 9.21cm

B. 9.15cm

C. 9.43cm

D. 9.76cm

QUESTION 7

Michael is saving money to buy his first house. Currently, Michael has $3,800 in his bank account. His bank account pays 5% compound interest each year. How much money will Michael have after 2 years?

A. $4198.50

B. $4189.80

C. $4089.50

D. $4189.50

QUESTION 8

Millie draws a triangle which has a base that is 3 cm longer than the height of the triangle. The area of the triangle is 150 cm². Work out the height of the triangle.

A. 8cm

B. 9cm

C. 10cm

D. 11cm

QUESTION 9

Work out the length of side A.

A. 16cm

B. 18cm

C. 20cm

D. 22cm

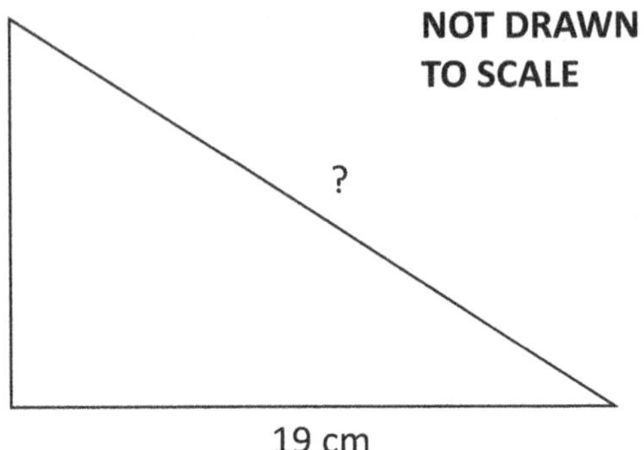

QUESTION 10

Work out the following:

$4\frac{2}{3} + 3\frac{1}{4}$. Write your answer as a mixed number.

A. $5\,{}^{11}\!/_{12}$

B. $7\,{}^{3}\!/_{4}$

C. $7\,{}^{1}\!/_{12}$

D. $7\,{}^{11}\!/_{12}$

QUESTION 11

For the expression, work out the value. Your answer should be given in standard form.

$10^{100} \times 4 \times 3 \times 10^{400}$

A	B	C	D
12×10^{300}	12×10^{500}	12×5^{500}	6×10^{500}

QUESTION 12

Using the diagram, calculate the perimeter of the lily bed.

A. 90 meters.

B. 40 meters.

C. 250 meters.

D. 2,800 meters.

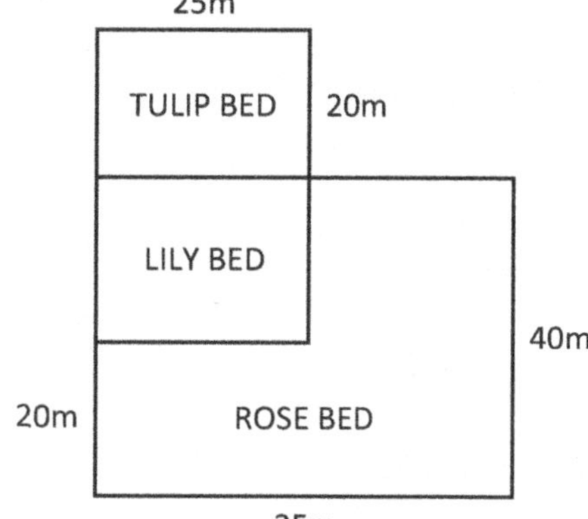

QUESTION 13

In July, Ryan worked a total of 40 hours. In August he worked 46.5 hours. By what percentage did Ryan's working hours increase in August?

A. 16.15%

B. 16.75%

C. 16.25%

D. 16.5%

QUESTION 14

Expand and simplify 8(2a + 8) + 4(9a − 3)

A	B	C	D
52(a + 52)	52a + 50	50a + 52	52a + 52

QUESTION 15

Samantha is a carpenter. She makes 3 oak tables for a family. The first table top measures 0.75 x 2 meters, the second measures 1.5 x 3 meters and the third measures 1 x 3 meters. What is the average area of the table tops?

A. 9 meters^2.

B. 3 meters^2.

C. 1.5 meters^2.

D. 4 meters^2.

QUESTION 16

Work out the volume of the prism.

A. 122cm^3

B. 144cm^3

C. 29cm^3

D. 98cm^3

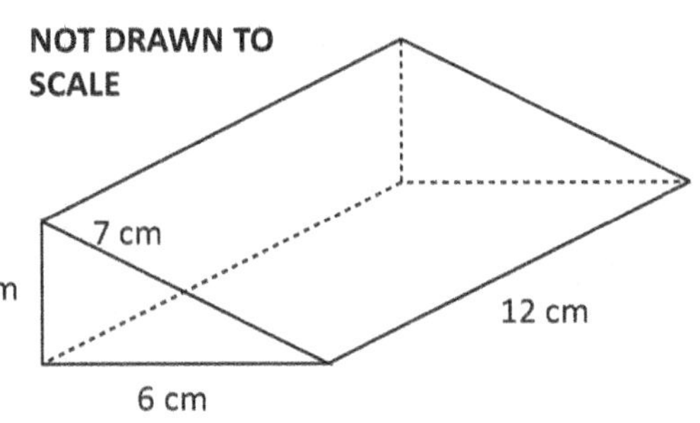

QUESTION 17

Multiply out 13a (2a − 5)

A	B	C	D
26a² - 65a	18a² - 65a	26a² - 55a	26a - 65a

QUESTION 18

Katie is given weekly pocket money for her part time jobs. Here is how much she earns across six weeks.

$40.60 $32.20 $75.80 $25.00 $15.50 $20.90

Work out the mean.

A. $15.75

B. $25

C. $25.50

D. $35

QUESTION 19

Look at the sequence below:

1   9   17   25   33   …   …

What are the next two terms in the sequence?

A	B	C	D
41 and 49	41 and 43	35 and 39	40 and 45

QUESTION 20

Simplify the expression:

$$13^9 \div 13^1$$

A	B	C	D
26^{10}	26^8	13^{10}	13^8

QUESTION 21

Calculate the exact value of $4.4^3 - 1.4^4$

A. 81.4324

B. 81.4424

C. 83.3424

D. 81.3424

QUESTION 22

Ollie and David are going on holiday. They need to change their British pounds into dollars. They have £1,340 to change into dollars with the exchange rate of £1 = \$1.36. Work out how many whole dollars they will have.

A	B	C	D
\$1822	\$1222	\$1882	\$1888

QUESTION 23

Work out the value of x:

$$4(3x + 15) = 3(5x + 17.5)$$

A	B	C	D
2.5	5	7.5	9

QUESTION 24

Solve the equation:

$$2(4b + 7) - 2b = 3(3b) - 10$$

A. b = 8

B. b = 4

C. b = 11

D. b = 12

QUESTION 25

Which two numbers come next in the sequence?

185   176   167   158   149

A	B	C	D
141 157	137 222	140 131	135 128

Electronics Information

You have **9** minutes to complete **20** questions.

QUESTION 1

What are the basic particles that make up an atom?

A. Protons, neutrons and particles.

B. Protons and electrons.

C. Neutrons, protons and electrons.

D. Mesons, neutrons and electrons.

QUESTION 2

Identify the following electrical symbol:

A. Diode.

B. Light dependent resistor.

C. Light emitting diode.

D. Variable resistor.

QUESTION 3

A bicycle uses a battery operated light for its front and rear lights. The front and rear lights are often of different sized bulbs. The filament in the rear lamp has a resistance of 4 ohms. It takes a current of 0.3 A. What voltage does the lamp work at?

A. 1.8 V.

B. 0.075 V.

C. 0.7 V.

D. 1.2 V.

QUESTION 4

Computer monitors and television screens are often covered in dust because…

A. The dust is attracted by the cool air of the technological device.

B. Dust is unmanageable.

C. The dust is attracted to the microfibers of the screen.

D. The dust is attracted by the static charges compelling from the technological device.

QUESTION 5

Electrical potential difference also means _________.

A	B	C	D
Current	Resistance	Voltage	Parallel circuit

QUESTION 6

The lines of magnetic flux tend to be considered as having what direction?

A. Towards a south pole.

B. Towards a north pole.

C. South to north outside of a magnet.

D. North to south outside of a magnet.

QUESTION 7

What is wrong with the circuit shown below?

A. It is an incomplete circuit.

B. The ammeter needs to be connected in series.

C. The ammeter needs to be a voltmeter instead.

D. There is only one ammeter.

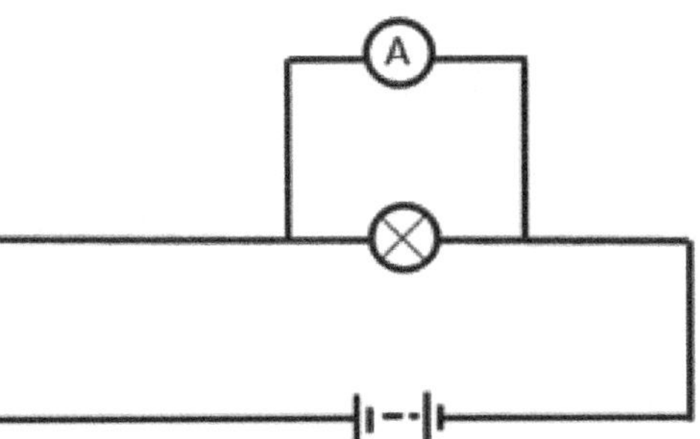

QUESTION 8

Current electricity occurs when _______ flow freely between more than one object.

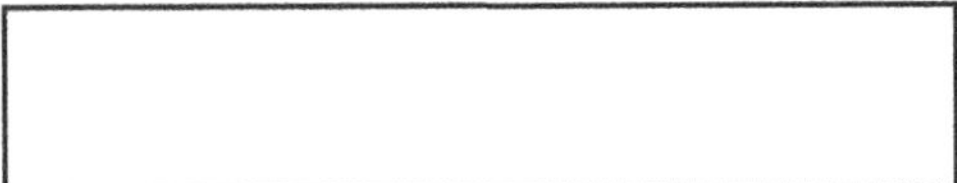

A	B	C	D
Resistance	Electrons	Neutrons	Voltage

QUESTION 9

A simple circuit contains a light bulb and a battery. The current through the battery is…

A. Less than the current through the light bulb.

B. More than the current through the light bulb.

C. The same as the current through the light bulb.

D. Less than the current through the path of wiring.

QUESTION 10

Birds can stand on high voltage electric power lines. They can do this safely. This is because …

A. The potential difference between the bird's feet is high.

B. They are aware of the power lines that are 'live', and those that are not.

C. The potential difference between the bird's feet is low.

D. They have complete resistance to the voltage.

QUESTION 11

What is the SI unit of capacitance?

A	B	C	D
Ohm	Farad	Amps	Joules

QUESTION 12

Removing the electrons from an atom would make the atom?

A. Positively charged.

B. A negative ion.

C. Negatively charged.

D. A positive ion.

QUESTION 13

Which electrical component is the following a description of...

As light intensity increases, the resistance goes down.

A. Light emitting diode.

B. Variable resistor.

C. Thermistor.

D. Light dependent resistor.

QUESTION 14

The potential difference across each branch within a parallel circuit is
________ as the potential difference across the source.

A	B	C	D
lowered	highered	the same	fluctuated

QUESTION 15

In electromagnets, the relationship between the electrical and magnetic waves will be…

A. Diagonal from one another.

B. In phase with one another.

C. Perpendicular with one another.

D. Unable to determine.

QUESTION 16

Which of the following devices converts alternating current supply to direct current supply?

A. Inverters.

B. Choppers.

C. Rectifiers.

D. Cannot be done.

QUESTION 17

On electrical equipment, where should the following symbol be included?

A	B	C	D
When earth bonding is not present in an electrical appliance.	When electrical appliances should not be exposed.	When electrical equipment has no insulation.	When electrical equipment has basic insulation only.

QUESTION 18

The electrical component zener diodes, is commonly used in…

A. Oscillator circuits.

B. Power supply circuits.

C. Current-limiting circuits.

D. Amplified circuits.

QUESTION 19

The root mean square (RMS) value in an alternating current circuit is…

A. The peak value of a square-wave system.

B. Seldom used because it is difficult to calculate.

C. The effective value which is almost always given.

D. The square root of the average value.

QUESTION 20

The formula for the power dissipated in the alternating current circuit which has a power factor of unity is called…

A	B	C	D
$P = V^2R$.	$P = I^2R$.	$P = VIR$.	$P = R \div V^2$.

Auto and Shop Information

You have **11** minutes to complete **25** questions.

QUESTION 1

What is the mechanical term for the equipment which mixes fuel with air?

A. Crankshaft.

B. Exhaust.

C. Carburetors.

D. Catalytic converter.

QUESTION 2

A mortising chisel is used to...

A. Create small, precise holes in metal.

B. Chisel away waste wood.

C. Used to install hinges.

D. Chisel away wallpaper and other thin materials.

QUESTION 3

Which of the following cutting tools would be best suited to cut curved lines?

A. Ripsaw.

B. Hacksaw.

C. Crosscut saw.

D. Coping saw.

QUESTION 4

Which of the following is NOT part of a cooling system?

A. Thermostat.

B. Hydrator.

C. Radiator.

D. Heater core.

QUESTION 5

The ground wire is always what colour?

A. White.

B. Green.

C. Black.

D. Blue

QUESTION 6

Which of the following is NOT part of an internal combustion engine?

A. Clutch.

B. Connecting rod.

C. Cylinder block.

D. Piston.

QUESTION 7

In a four-stroke engine system, what order would the following be arranged in?

A. Intake, power, exhaust and compression.

B. Power, intake, exhaust and compression.

C. Intake, compression, exhaust and power.

D. Intake, compression, power and exhaust.

QUESTION 8

What is the inner edge of a tire called?

A. Sidewall.

B. Bead.

C. Rim.

D. Nylon belt.

QUESTION 9

What is the best definition of a car tread?

A. The metal rim around the tyre to keep the tire firmly on the ground.

B. The rubber on the tire that counts how many times the wheel rotates.

C. The rubber on the tire which makes contact with the road, and is gradually worn off.

D. All of the above.

QUESTION 10

A connecting rod connects the piston to what?

A. Exhaust.

B. Crankshaft.

C. Radiator.

D. Cylinder head.

QUESTION 11

How can you tell if you are using the right octane level?

A. If the car does make a knocking sound, then you're using the right amount.

B. If the car makes sudden judders when braking, then you're using the right amount.

C. If the car doesn't make a knocking sound, then you're using the right amount.

D. None of the above.

QUESTION 12

Which of the following fastening tools is best used for turning screws with a blade shaped like a cross?

A. Allen wrench.

B. Open-end wrench.

C. Standard screwdriver.

D. Phillips screwdriver.

QUESTION 13

Which of the following definitions best describes a plumb bob?

A. A gripping tool suspended from a line.

B. A large ruler to measure water.

C. A measuring tool used to check the accuracy of an angle.

D. A heavy weight suspended from a line.

QUESTION 14

An elevator is most similar to which of the following mechanical devices?

A	B	C	D
Spring	Hydraulic jet	Lever	Crane

QUESTION 15

A screw has 8 threads per inch. How many full turns are required for the nut to travel 3 inches?

A	B	C	D
8 turns	12 turns	16 turns	24 turns

QUESTION 16

Electric-arc welding produces...

A. Ultraviolet radiation.

B. Microwave radiation.

C. Gamma radiation.

D. Beta radiation.

QUESTION 17

Engine displacement can...

A. Increase the car's toxic emissions.

B. Reduce fuel efficiency and power.

C. Increase tire pressure.

D. Reduce brake time efficiency.

QUESTION 18

Generally, disc brakes can usually be located...

A. On the front wheels.

B. On the back wheels.

C. In the engine.

D. In the handbrake system.

QUESTION 19

Apart from disconnecting the engine from the drive shaft, the clutch also...

A. Allows the engine to turn efficiently in terms of fumes.

B. Allows the driver to reduce their speed when required.

C. Allows the wheels to maintain balance when the car is in motion.

D. Allows the engine to run when the car is not in motion.

QUESTION 20

Which of the following clamping tools should you use if you want to drill through a piece of wood?

A. Pliers.

B. Vise.

C. C-clamps.

D. Any of the above.

QUESTION 21

The tool pictured is a...

A. Vise grip plier.

B. C-clamp.

C. Socket wrench.

D. Calliper.

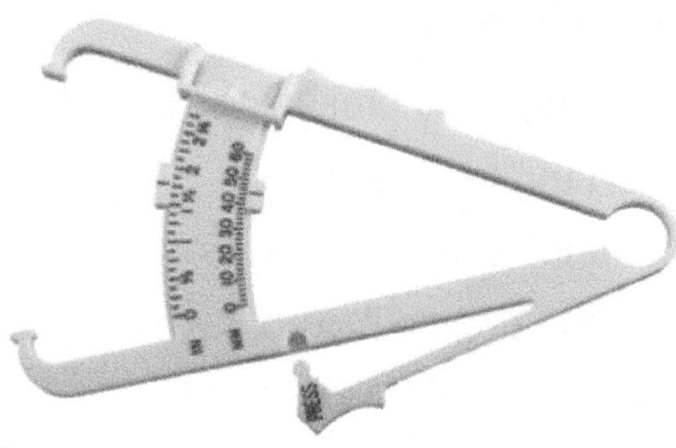

QUESTION 22

The tool pictured is a...

A. Disc brake.

B. Drum brakes.

C. Wing nut.

D. Brake pedal.

QUESTION 23

The tool pictured is a...

A. Washer.

B. Wing nut.

C. Rivet.

D. Bolt.

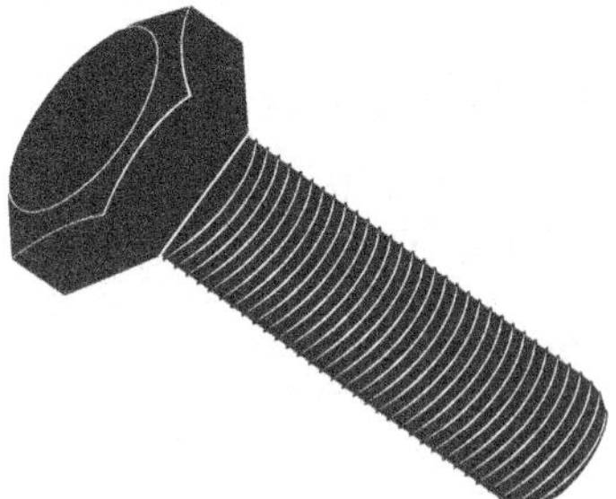

QUESTION 24

Cap nuts are...

A. Used to prevent screws or bolts from loosening.

B. Smooth and round in shape.

C. Used to fasten metal pieces together.

D. Square or hexagonal in shape.

QUESTION 25

After filling in a hole using plastic filler, what should you do next?

A. Sand down the area with sandpaper.

B. Paint over the area with oil-based paint.

C. Clean the area using a small chisel and some boiling water.

D. None of the above.

Mechanical Comprehension

You have **19** minutes to complete **25** questions.

QUESTION 1

What does Pascal's Law deal with?

A. The pressure at the bottom of a container.

B. The amplification of force in a hydraulic system.

C. The mechanical advantage of a pulley system.

D. The flow of liquid from one container to another.

QUESTION 2

LEDs are being used more and more. What logical explanation can be used to determine why this might be?

A. They have a higher resistance.

B. They require a higher voltage.

C. They are more eco-friendly.

D. They provide a higher current.

QUESTION 3

Which of the following best describes the type of machine shown below?

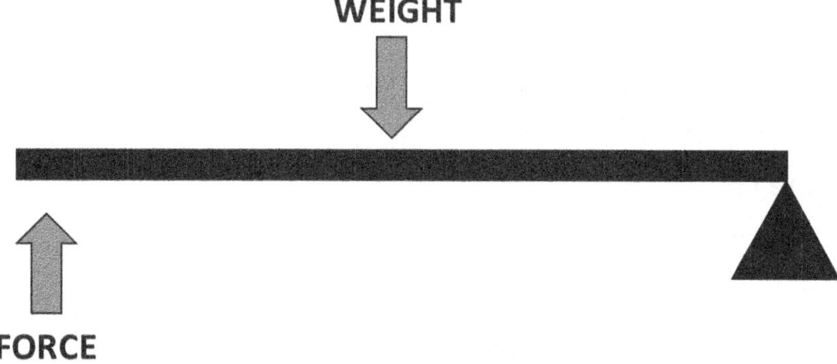

A	B	C	D
Third-class lever	First-class lever	Pulley system	Second-class lever

QUESTION 4

In order to lift the 3,000-pound weight, approximately how many pounds would you need to pull down with?

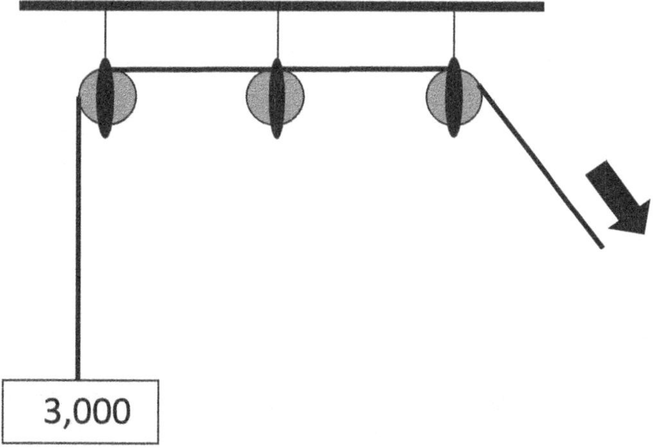

A	B	C	D
1,000	500	3,000	50

QUESTION 5

Imagine this scenario. You live at one end of the city. A huge thunderstorm is heading your way. Lightning strikes at the other end of the city.

What do you think you would experience first: hearing the thunder or seeing the lightning?

A. See the lightning.

B. Hear the thunder.

C. See and hear at the same time.

QUESTION 6

__________________ are a form of wasteful circulation currents which are observed in iron cores, which result in loss of energy.

A. Core currents

B. Hysteresis currents

C. Neutral currents

D. Eddy currents

QUESTION 7

The opposite of a current flow in an alternating current resistive circuit is…

A	B	C	D
Resistance	Impedance	Reactance	Inductance

QUESTION 8

If a person uses 500 Newtons of force across a distance of 150 meters, how many Joules of work is performed?

A	B	C	D
20	1,000	75,000	7,000

QUESTION 9

If a drawing is not drawn to the full size, the scale of the drawing will be indicated. What does the scale '1:6' indicate?

A. 1 cm on the drawing represents 6 cm on the component.

B. 1 cm on the drawing represents 6 meters on the component.

C. 6 cm on the drawing represents 1 cm on the component.

D. The drawing is 6 times the size of the full size drawing.

QUESTION 10

Michael wants to connect an electrolytic capacitor in a circuit. An electrolytic capacitor is a type of capacitor that generates larger capacitance by using electrolytes. Michael is a professor in physics. He knows the important relationship of connecting an electrolytic capacitor in the correct polarity. Out of the following explanations, which best describes the probable result if an electrolytic capacitor is connected with the wrong polarity?

A. The capacitance will decrease.

B. The capacitor will burst.

C. The capacitance will increase.

D. There will be no noticeable effect.

QUESTION 11

If electricity costs 8 cents per unit and a 6 kW appliance runs for approximately 75 minutes, what is the total cost?

A	B	C	D
$3,600	$9.80	$48.00	$36.00

QUESTION 12

If gear A in the diagram begins spinning clockwise, what will happen to the spring that is attached to the wall?

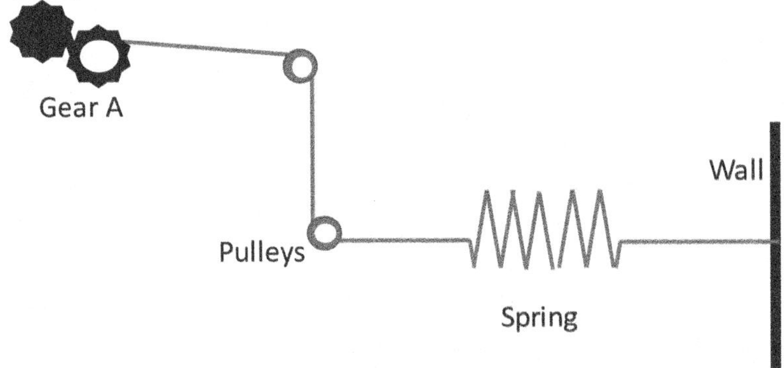

A	B	C	D
The spring will be compressed	The spring will stretch	The spring will touch the gears	Nothing

QUESTION 13

An aircraft with a mass of 1,600 kilograms starts at rest and accelerates along a horizontal runway. The engine of the aircraft produces a constant thrust of 4,200 N. There is a constant frictional force of 300 N which is acting on the aircraft.

What is the acceleration of the aircraft?

A	B	C	D
24.75 ms^{-2}	4.2652 ms^{-2}	2.4375 ms^{-2}	3.1354 ms^{-2}

QUESTION 14

Water is flowing into the following tank through the left-hand side inlet pipe at a rate of 18 liters per minute. If the water is flowing out through the lower right-hand side outlet pipe at a rate of 14 liters per minute, approximately how much time will it take for the tank to overflow?

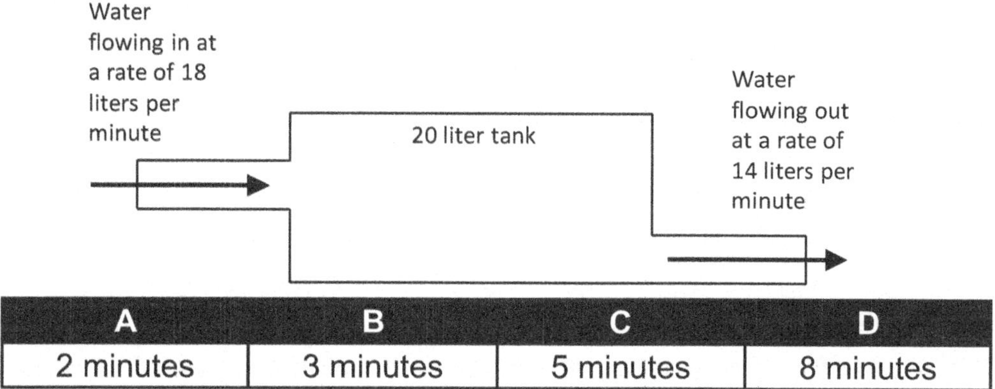

A	B	C	D
2 minutes	3 minutes	5 minutes	8 minutes

QUESTION 15

A hot air balloon is able to float because:

A. The hot air is turbo-charged

B. The hot air is less dense than the external air

C. The hot air is denser than the external air

D. It is filled with helium

QUESTION 16

Why does an astronaut weigh less on the Moon than on Earth?

A	B	C
The force of gravity is weaker on the Moon.	The force of gravity is weaker on Earth.	The Moon has no gravity.

QUESTION 17

Which of the following equations would you use to work out the voltage?

A. Voltage = current ÷ resistance

B. Voltage = resistance ÷ current

C. Voltage = current x resistance

D. Voltage = power x resistance

QUESTION 18

What transfers from a carpet made from nylon to give off a static electrical shock?

A	B	C	D
Nucleus	Protons	Electrons	Atoms

QUESTION 19

When a cloth is rubbed against an object made of copper, no charge happens because...

A. Copper is a conductor.

B. Copper is an insulator.

C. The cloth is not electronically charged.

D. It is a brittle metal.

QUESTION 20

The total current flowing through the circuit below is…

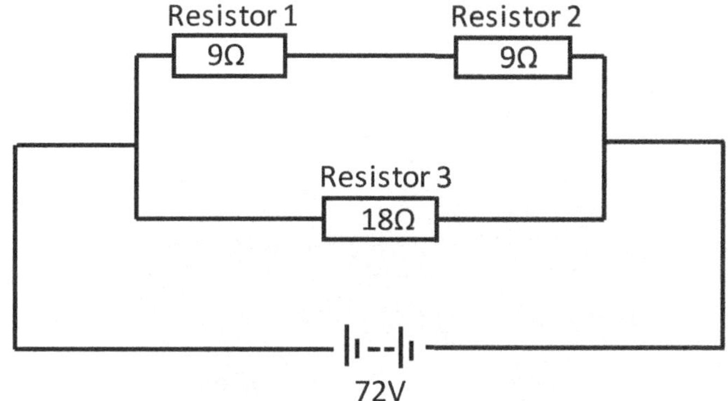

A	B	C	D
4A	8A	16A	18A

QUESTION 21

If cog A turns anti-clockwise, which way will cog C turn?

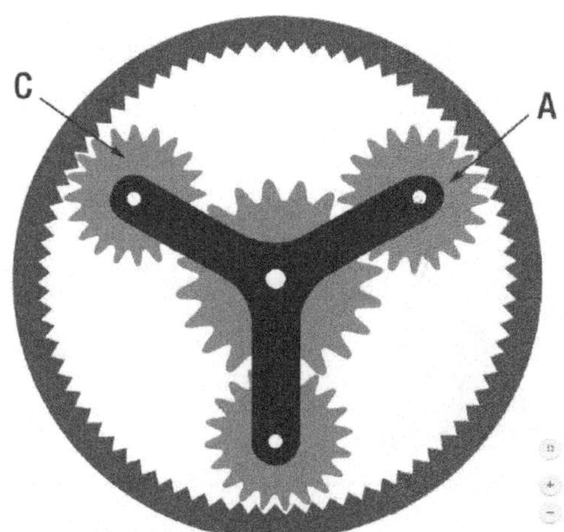

A	B	C
Clockwise	Anti-clockwise	Backwards and forwards

QUESTION 22

What will happen to the air resistance on a car as the car picks up speed?

A	B	C
The air resistance will increase	The air resistance will decrease	The air resistance will stay the same

QUESTION 23

How much weight is required to balance point X?

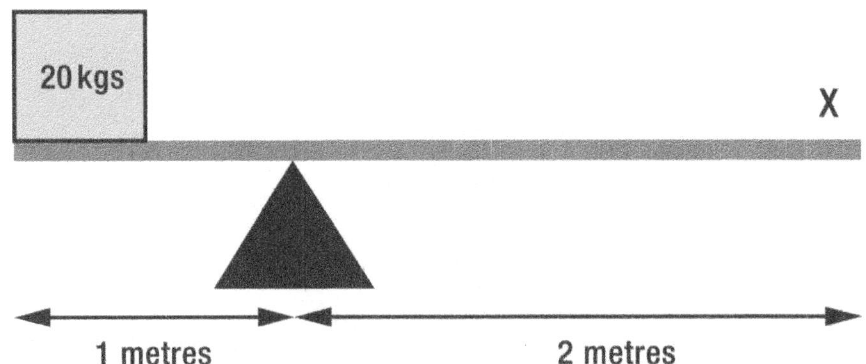

A	B	C	D
5 kg	10 kg	15 kg	20 kg

QUESTION 24

The process of extracting or refining a substance via boiling and condensation. This process is also known as...

A. Concurrent.

B. Distillation.

C. Hydraulics.

D. Reaction forces.

QUESTION 25

Using a runner gives you a mechanical advantage of what?

A. 0

B. 1

C. 2

D. 4

Assembling Objects

You have **15** minutes to complete **25** questions.

QUESTION 1

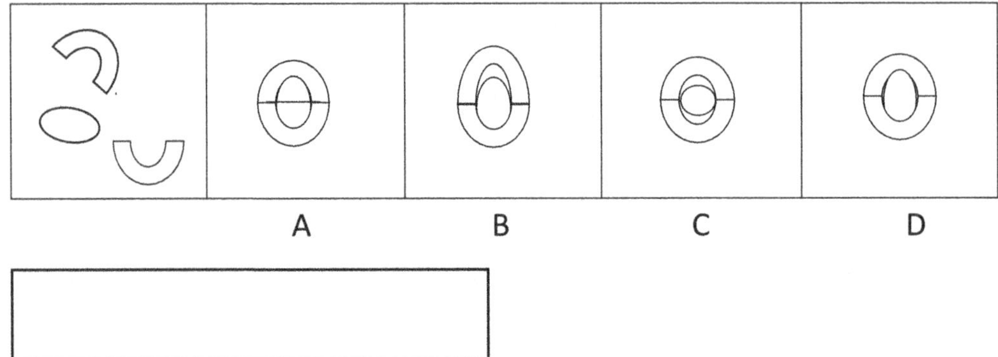

QUESTION 2

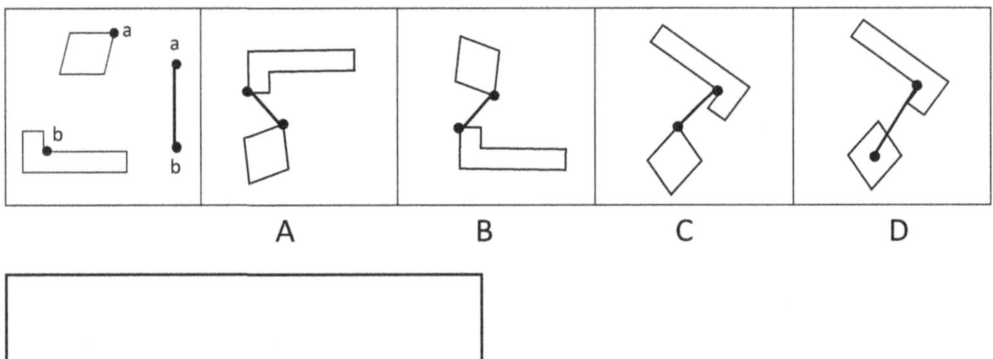

QUESTION 3

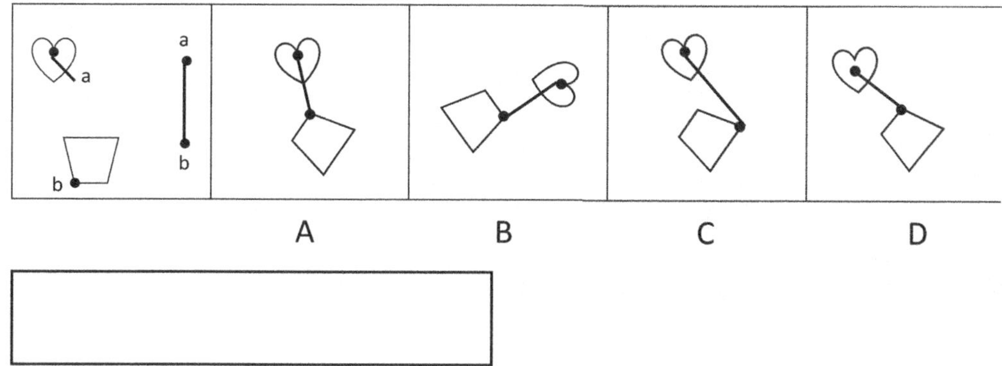

QUESTION 4

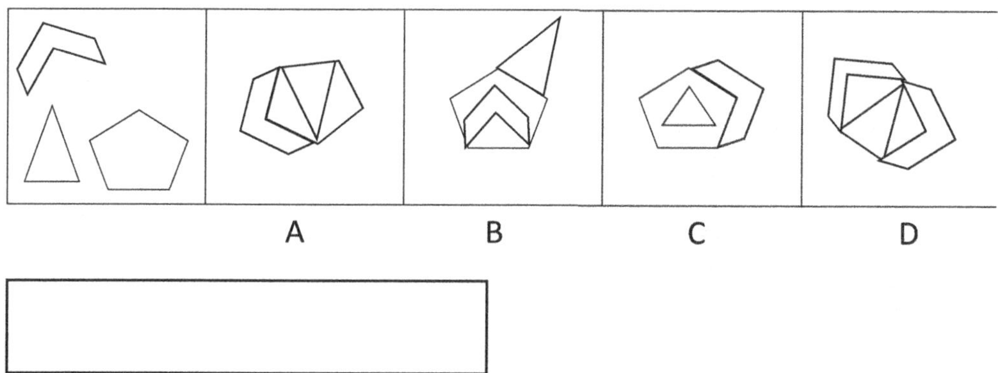

QUESTION 5

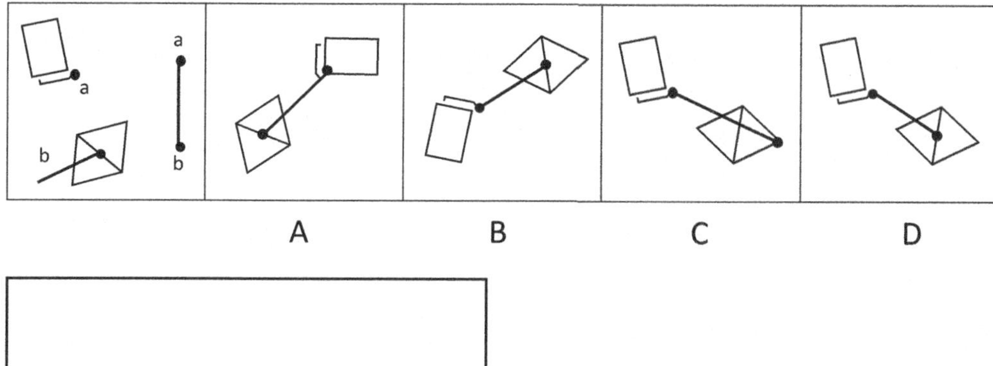

QUESTION 6

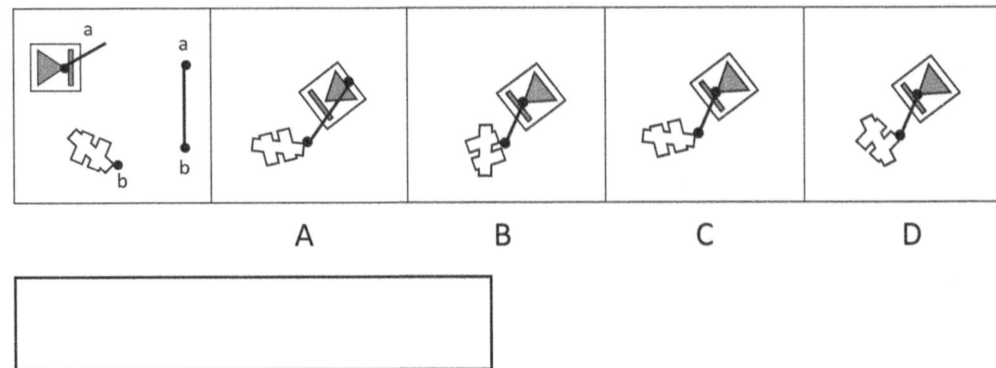

QUESTION 7

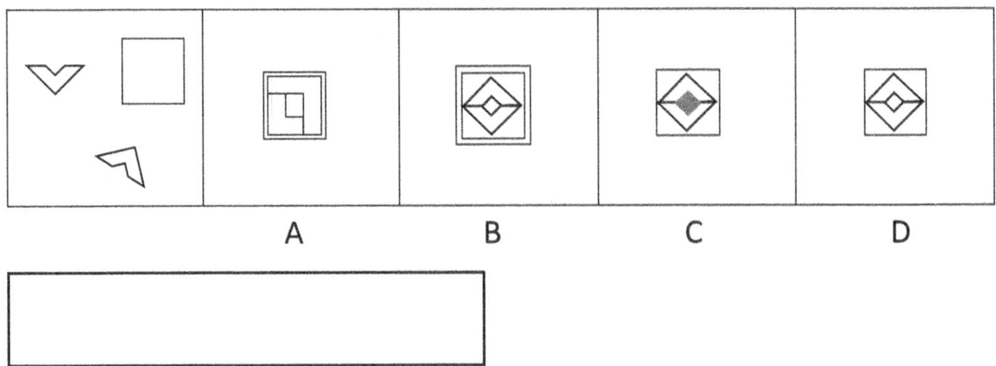

QUESTION 8

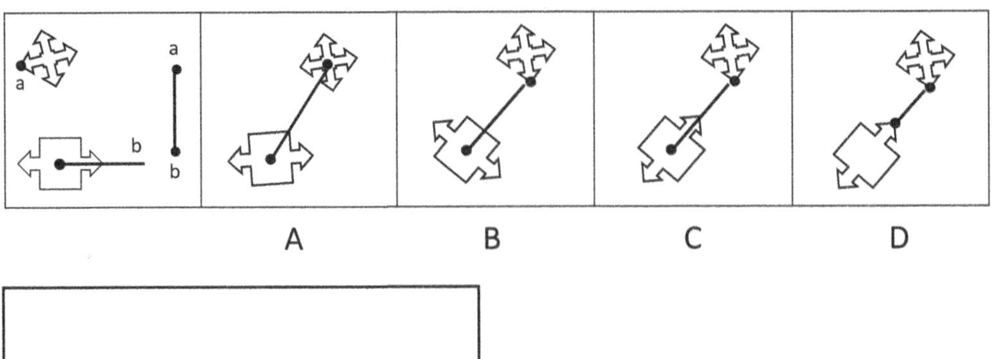

QUESTION 9

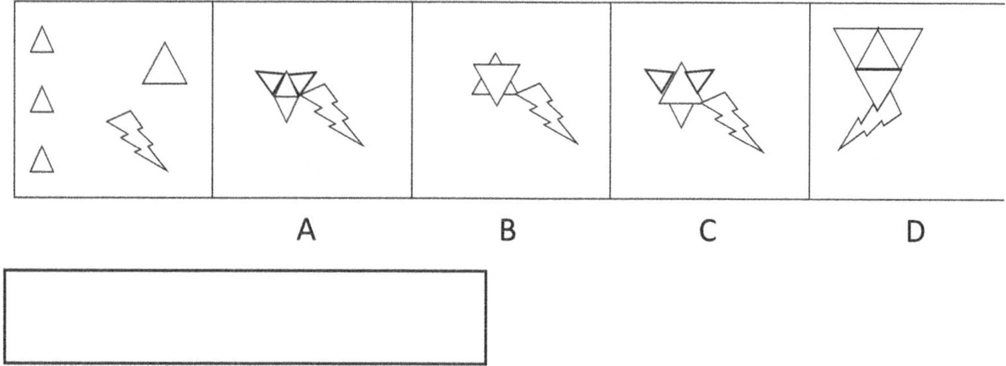

QUESTION 10

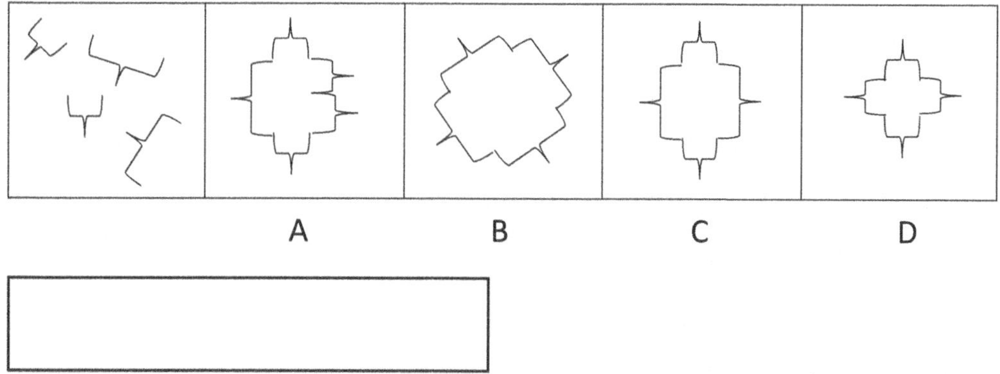

QUESTION 11

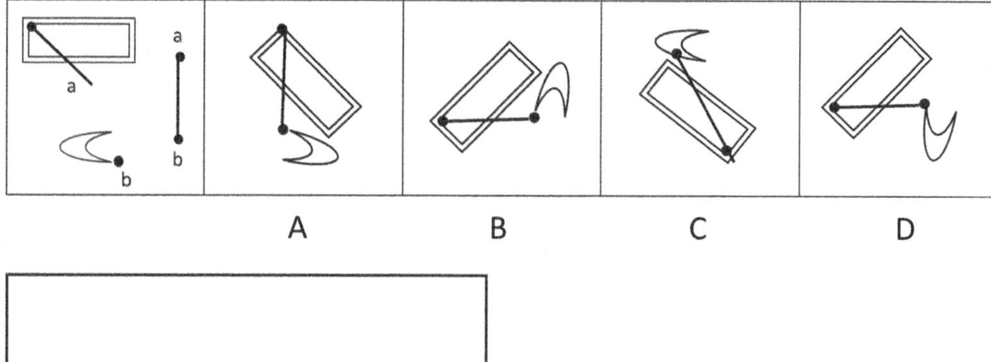

QUESTION 12

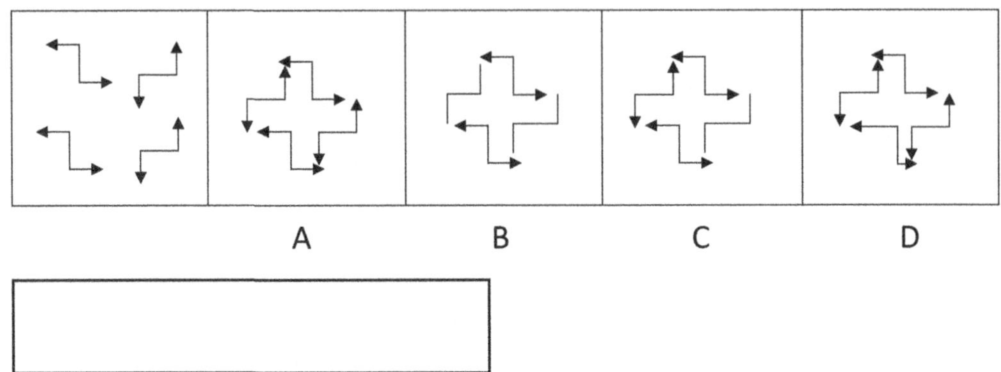

QUESTION 13

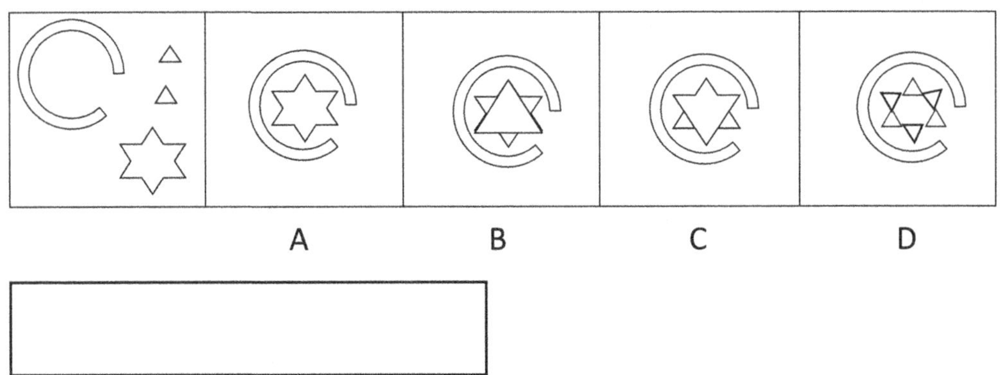

QUESTION 14

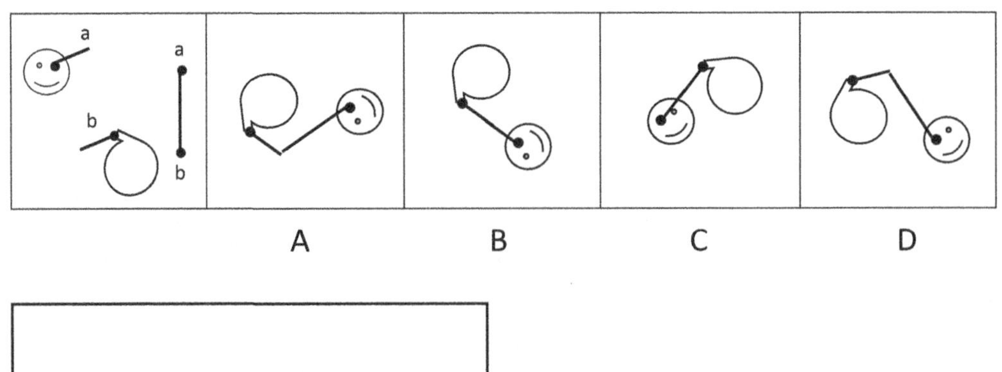

QUESTION 15

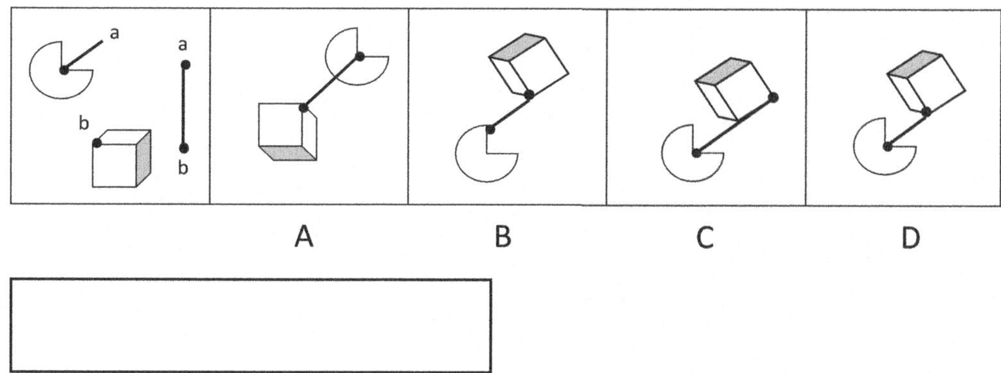

A   B   C   D

QUESTION 16

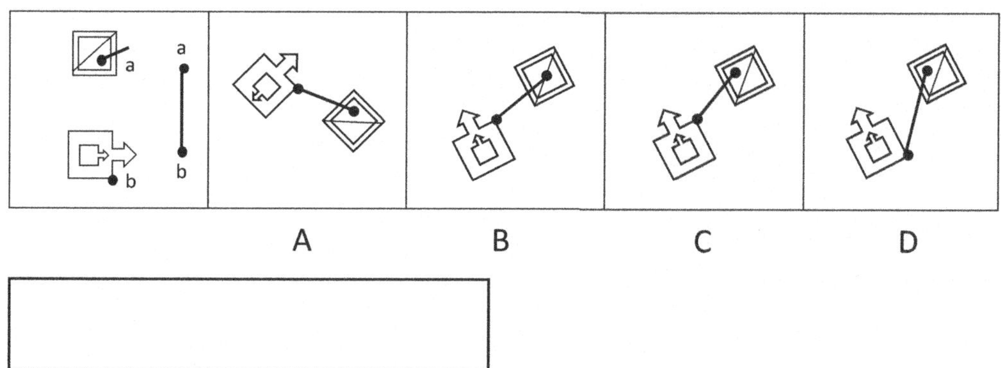

A   B   C   D

QUESTION 17

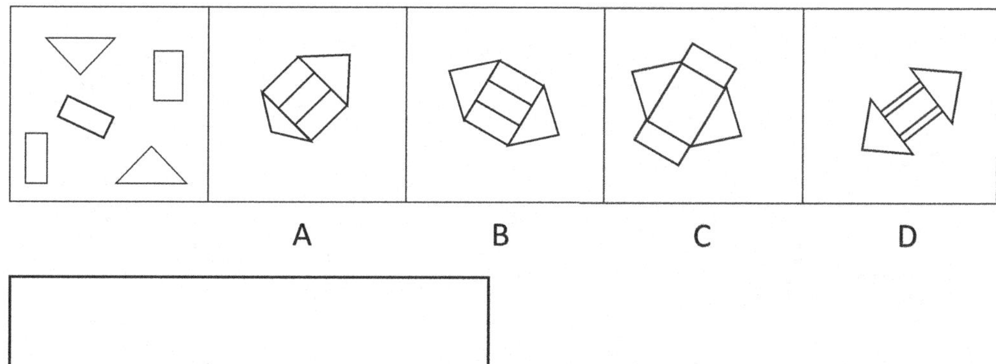

A   B   C   D

QUESTION 18

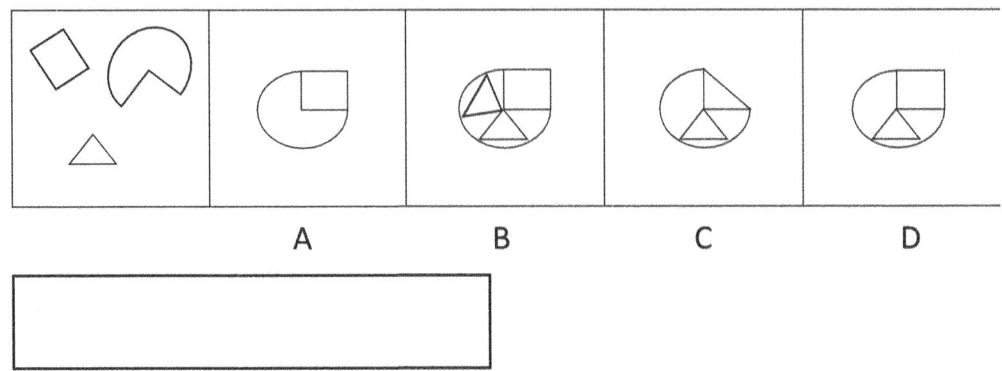

A   B   C   D

QUESTION 19

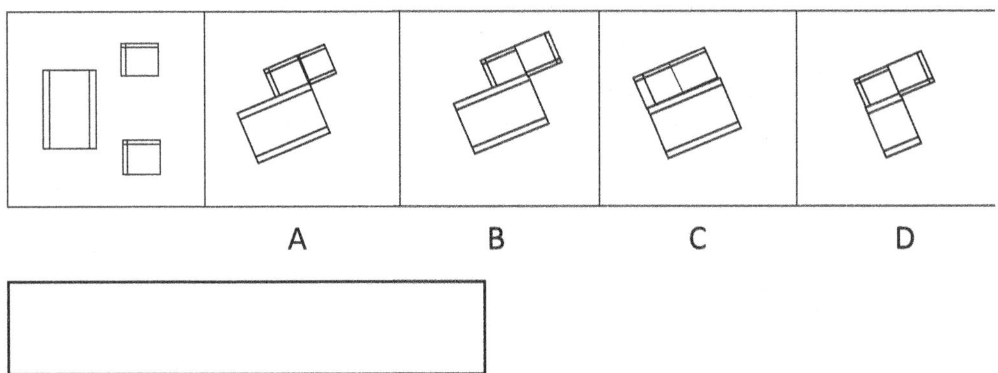

A   B   C   D

QUESTION 20

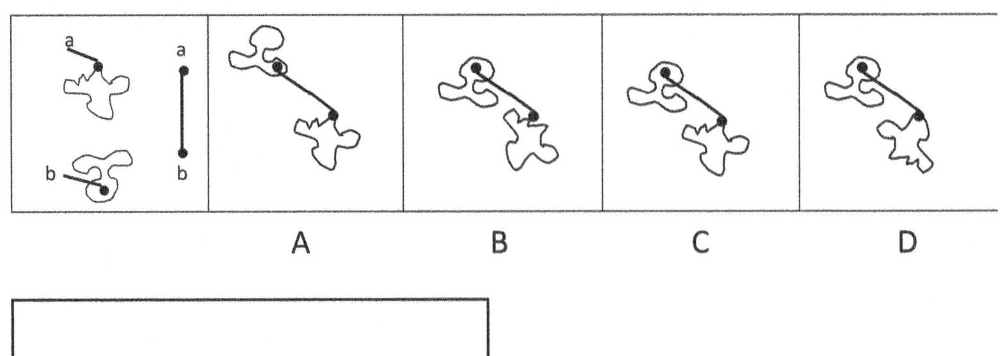

A   B   C   D

QUESTION 21

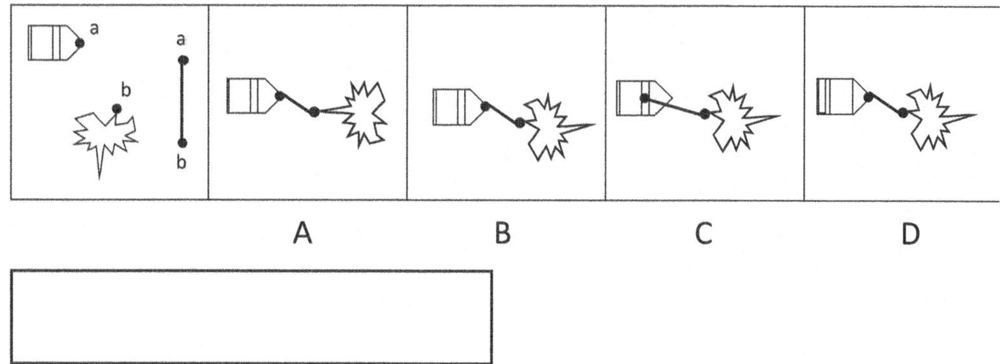

QUESTION 22

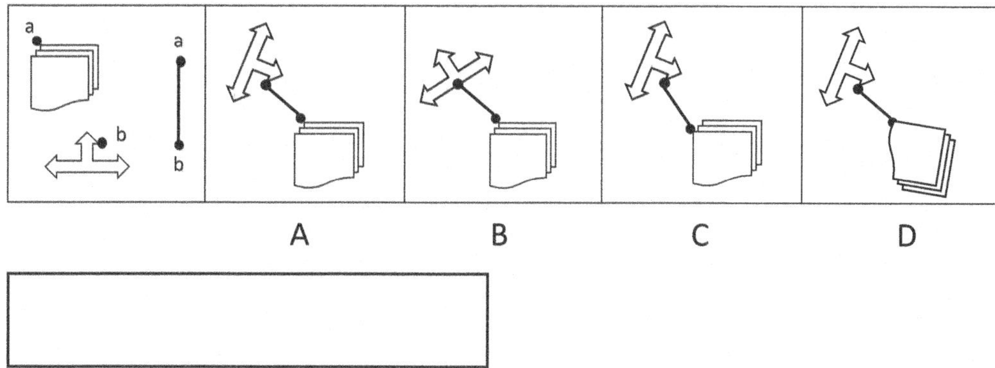

QUESTION 23

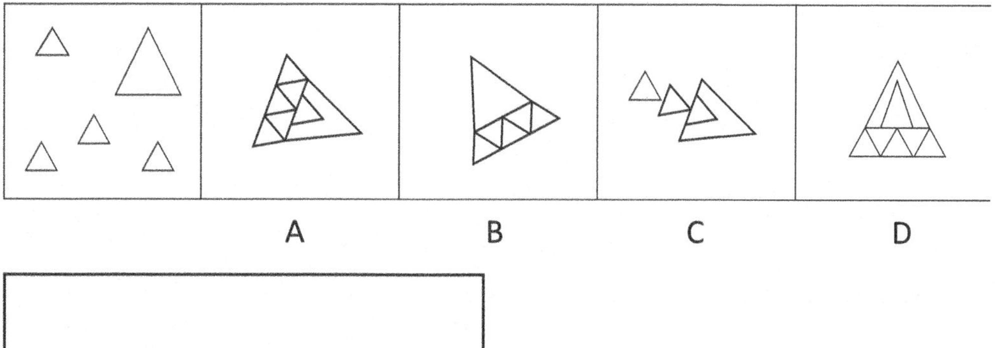

264 ASVAB

QUESTION 24

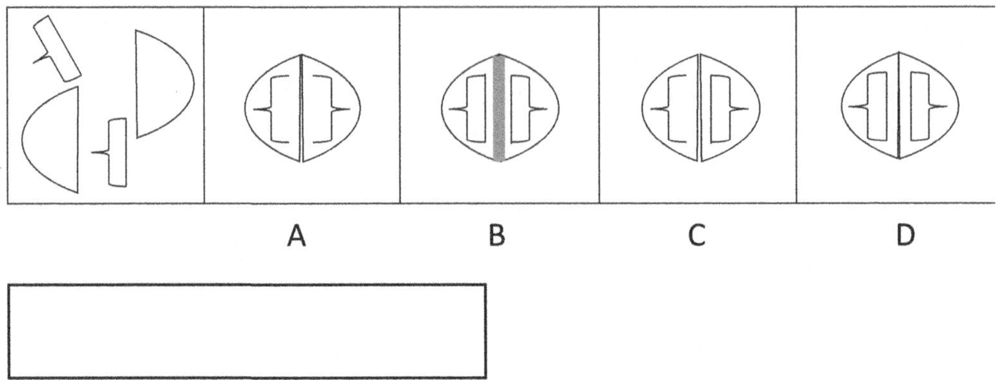

A   B   C   D

QUESTION 25

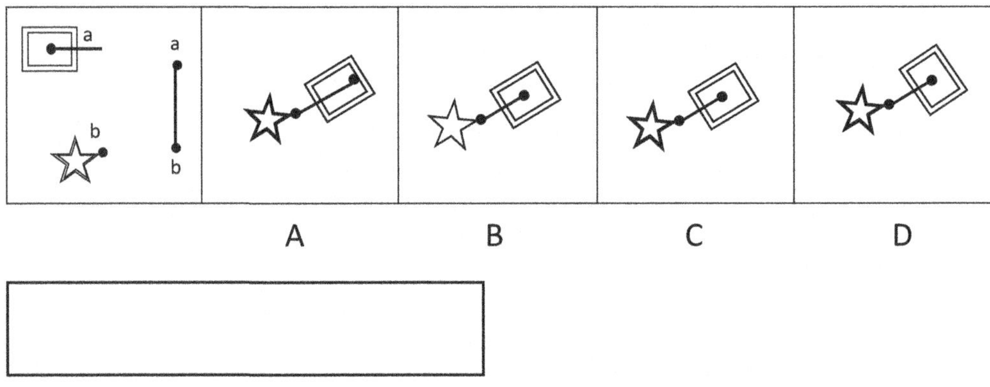

A   B   C   D

ANSWERS TO ASVAB PRACTICE TEST

GENERAL SCIENCE	ARITHMETIC REASONING	
Q1. B	Q1. C	Q26. D
Q2. C	Q2. A	Q27. C
Q3. A	Q3. C	Q28. A
Q4. C	Q4. C	Q29. B
Q5. A	Q5. D	Q30. C
Q6. D	Q6. A	
Q7. B	Q7. D	
Q8. D	Q8. B	
Q9. B	Q9. A	
Q10. A	Q10. C	
Q11. D	Q11. B	
Q12. C	Q12. A	
Q13. D	Q13. B	
Q14. D	Q14. B	
Q15. C	Q15. C	
Q16. A	Q16. C	
Q17. C	Q17. A	
Q18. B	Q18. D	
Q19. A	Q19. C	
Q20. C	Q20. C	
Q21. A	Q21. A	
Q22. D	Q22. B	
Q23. A	Q23. D	
Q24. C	Q24. C	
Q25. C	Q25. B	

WORD KNOWLEDGE		PARAGRAPH COMPREHENSION
Q1. A	Q26. D	Q1. D
Q2. D	Q27. D	Q2. A
Q3. C	Q28. C	Q3. C
Q4. C	Q29. A	Q4. D
Q5. D	Q30. A	Q5. B
Q6. D	Q31. C	Q6. B
Q7. D	Q32. B	Q7. D
Q8. D	Q33. A	Q8. A
Q9. C	Q34. C	Q9. C
Q10. B	Q35. B	Q10. B
Q11. B		Q11. C
Q12. A		Q12. B
Q13. C		Q13. A
Q14. D		Q14. D
Q15. D		Q15. C
Q16. B		
Q17. D		
Q18. A		
Q19. C		
Q20. D		
Q21. C		
Q22. B		
Q23. D		
Q24. A		
Q25. D		

MATHEMATICS KNOWLEDGE	ELECTRONICS INFORMATION
Q1. A	Q1. C
Q2. C	Q2. C
Q3. A	Q3. D
Q4. A	Q4. D
Q5. C	Q5. C
Q6. C	Q6. D
Q7. D	Q7. B
Q8. C	Q8. B
Q9. D	Q9. C
Q10. D	Q10. C
Q11. B	Q11. B
Q12. A	Q12. D
Q13. C	Q13. D
Q14. D	Q14. C
Q15. B	Q15. C
Q16. B	Q16. C
Q17. A	Q17. D
Q18. D	Q18. B
Q19. A	Q19. C
Q20. D	Q20. B
Q21. D	
Q22. A	
Q23. A	
Q24. A	
Q25. C	

AUTO AND SHOP INFORMATION	MECHANICAL COMPREHENSION
Q1. C	Q1. B
Q2. B	Q2. C
Q3. D	Q3. D
Q4. B	Q4. C
Q5. B	Q5. A
Q6. A	Q6. D
Q7. D	Q7. A
Q8. B	Q8. C
Q9. C	Q9. A
Q10. B	Q10. B
Q11. C	Q11. D
Q12. D	Q12. A
Q13. D	Q13. C
Q14. D	Q14. C
Q15. D	Q15. B
Q16. A	Q16. A
Q17. B	Q17. C
Q18. A	Q18. C
Q19. D	Q19. A
Q20. B	Q20. B
Q21. D	Q21. B
Q22. A	Q22. A
Q23. D	Q23. B
Q24. B	Q24. B
Q25. A	Q25. C

ASSEMBLING OBJECTS

Q1. D

Q2. C

Q3. B

Q4. A

Q5. D

Q6. C

Q7. D

Q8. C

Q9. C

Q10. C

Q11. B

Q12. A

Q13. B

Q14. B

Q15. D

Q16. C

Q17. B

Q18. D

Q19. B

Q20. C

Q21. B

Q22. A

Q23. A

Q24. D

Q25. C

APPENDIX A

ALABAMA

MONTGOMERY, AL

Maxwell Air Force Base - Gunter Annex

705 McDonald Street

Bldg. 1512

Montgomery, AL 36114-3110

ALASKA

ANCHORAGE, AK

1717 "C" Street

Anchorage, AK 99501

ARIZONA

PHOENIX, AZ

1 North 1st Street

Suite 613

Phoenix, AZ 85004-2357

ARKANSAS

LITTLE ROCK, AR

1520 Riverfront Drive

Little Rock, AR 72202-1724

CALIFORNIA

LOS ANGELES, CA

1776 Grand Avenue

El Segundo, CA 90245

CALIFORNIA

SACRAMENTO, CA

3870 Rosin Court

Suite 105

Sacramento, CA 95834-1648

CALIFORNIA

SAN DIEGO, CA

4181 Ruffin Rd

Suite B

San Diego, CA 92123

CALIFORNIA

SAN JOSE, CA

546 Vernon Avenue

Mountain View, CA 94043

COLORADO

DENVER, CO

621 17th Street

Suite 479

Denver, CO 80293-0621

FLORIDA

JACKSONVILLE, FL

7178 Baymeadows Way

Jacksonville, FL 32256

FLORIDA

MIAMI, FL

7789 NW 48th Street

Suite 150

Miami, FL 33166

FLORIDA

TAMPA, FL

3520 West Waters Avenue

Tampa, FL 33614-2716

GEORGIA

ATLANTA, GA

1500 Hood Avenue

Building 720

Fort Gillem, GA 30297-5000

HAWAII

HONOLULU, HI

490 Central Avenue

Pearl Harbor, HI 96860

IDAHO

BOISE, ID

550 West Fort Street

MSC 044

Boise, ID 83724-0101

ILLINOIS

CHICAGO, IL

1700 South Wolf Road

Des Plaines, IL 60018

INDIANA

INDIANAPOLIS, IN

5541 Herbert Lord Drive

Indianapolis, IN 46216

IOWA

DES MOINES, IA

7105 NW 70th Avenue

Building S-71

Johnston, IA 50131

KENTUCKY

LOUISVILLE, KY 600

Dr. Martin Luther King, Jr., Place

Room 477

Louisville, KY 40202

LOUISIANA

NEW ORLEANS, LA

Belle Chasse Naval Air Station

400 Russell Avenue

New Orleans, LA 70143-5077

LOUISIANA

SHREVEPORT, LA

2715 Alkay Drive

Shreveport, LA 71118-2509

MAINE

PORTLAND, ME

510 Congress Street

3rd Floor

Portland, ME 04101-3403

MARYLAND

BALTIMORE, MD

850 Chisholm Avenue

Fort Meade, MD 20755

MASSACHUSETTS

BOSTON, MA

Barnes Building

495 Summer Street

4th Floor

Boston, MA 02210

MASSACHUSETTS

SPRINGFIELD, MA

551 Airlift Drive

Westover JARB

Springfield, MA 01022-1519

MICHIGAN

DETROIT, MI

1172 Kirts Boulevard

Troy, MI 48084-4846

MINNESOTA

MINNEAPOLIS, MN

212 3rd Ave. South

Minneapolis, MN 55401-2556

MISSISSIPPI

JACKSON, MS

664 South State Street

Jackson, MS 39201

MISSOURI

KANSAS CITY, MO

10316 NW Prairie View Road

Kansas City, MO 64153-1350

MISSOURI

ST. LOUIS, MO

Robert A. Young Federal Building

1222 Spruce Street

St. Louis, MO 63103-2816

MONTANA

BUTTE, MT

22 W. Park Street

Butte, MT 59701

NEBRASKA

OMAHA, NE

5303 "F" Street

Omaha, NE 68117-2805

NEW JERSEY

FORT DIX, NJ Building

5645 Texas Avenue

Fort Dix, NJ 08640

NEW MEXICO

ALBUQUERQUE, NM

505 Central Ave NW

Suite A

Albuquerque, NM 87102-2113

NEW YORK

ALBANY, NY

Leo W. O'Brien Federal Building

N. Pearl St & Clinton Avenue

Albany, NY 12207

NEW YORK

BUFFALO, NY

2024 Ent Ave, Building 799

Niagara Falls ARS, NY 14304-5000

NEW YORK

NEW YORK, NY

Fort Hamilton Military Community

116 White Avenue

Brooklyn, NY 11252-4705

NEW YORK

SYRACUSE, NY

6001 East Molloy Road

Building 710

Syracuse, NY 13211-2100

NORTH CAROLINA

CHARLOTTE, NC

6125 Tyvola Centre

Charlotte, NC 28217-6447

NORTH CAROLINA

RALEIGH, NC

2625 Appliance Court

Raleigh, NC 27604

NORTH DAKOTA

FARGO, ND

225 Fourth Avenue North

Fargo, ND 58102

OHIO

CLEVELAND, OH 20637

Emerald Parkway Drive

Cleveland, OH 44135-6023

OHIO

COLUMBUS, OH

775 Taylor Road

Gahanna, OH 43230

OKLAHOMA

OKLAHOMA CITY, OK

301 Northwest 6th Street

Suite 150

Oklahoma City, OK 73102

OREGON

PORTLAND, OR

7545 NE Ambassador Place

Portland, OR 97220-1367

PENNSYLVANIA

HARRISBURG, PA

4641 Westport Drive

Mechanicsburg, PA 17055

PENNSYLVANIA

PITTSBURGH, PA

William S. Moorhead Federal Building

1000 Liberty Avenue

Suite 1917

Pittsburgh, PA 15222-4101

PUERTO RICO

SAN JUAN, PR

651 Federal Drive

Ste. 113-19

Catano, PR 00962-5201

SOUTH CAROLINA

FORT JACKSON, SC

2435 Marion Avenue

Fort Jackson, SC 29207

SOUTH DAKOTA

SIOUX FALLS, SD

2801 South Kiwanis Avenue

Suite 200

Sioux Falls, SD 57105

TENNESSEE

KNOXVILLE, TN

9745 Parkside Drive

Knoxville, TN 37922

MEMPHIS

TN 480 Beale Street

Memphis, TN 38103-3232

NASHVILLE

TN 20 Bridgestone Park

Nashville, TN 37214-2428

TEXAS

AMARILLO, TX

1100 South Fillmore

Suite 100

Amarillo, TX 79101

TEXAS

DALLAS, TX

Federal Building

207 South Houston Street

Suite 400

Dallas, TX 75202

TEXAS

EL PASO, TX

6380 Morgan Avenue

Suite E

El Paso, TX 79906-4611

TEXAS

HOUSTON, TX

701 San Jacinto Street

PO Box #52309

Houston, TX 77052-2309

TEXAS

SAN ANTONIO, TX

2850 Stanley Rd

Suite 103

Ft. Sam Houston, TX 78234-2712

UTAH

SALT LAKE CITY, UT

2830 South Redwood Road

Salt Lake City, UT 84119-2375

VIRGINIA

FORT LEE, VA

2011 Mahone Avenue

Fort Lee, VA 23801-1707

WASHINGTON

SEATTLE, WA

4735 East Marginal Way South

Seattle, WA 98134-2385

WASHINGTON

SPOKANE, WA

8510 W. Highway 2

Spokane, WA 99224

WEST VIRGINIA

BECKLEY, WV

409 Wood Mountain Road

Glen Jean, WV 25846

WISCONSIN

MILWAUKEE, WI 11050

West Liberty Drive

Milwaukee, WI 53224

APPENDIX B

ACUTE ANGLES	An angle less than 90°.
ALGEBRA	The part of maths where symbols and letters are used to represent numbers.
AREA	A measurement of a surface. For the area of a square, you would multiply the height by the width.
BIDMAS	**B**rackets, **I**ndices, **D**ivision, **M**ultiplication, **A**ddition, **S**ubtraction – order of operations.
CIRCUMFERENCE	The distance around something. It is the enclosing boundary of a curved geometric figure.
COMPOUND SHAPE	A compound shape includes two or more simple shapes.
CUBED NUMBERS	A cubed number is a number multiplied by itself, three times.
DECIMAL PLACES	The position of a digit to the right of a decimal point.
DECIMAL	A type of number, for example 0.5 is equivalent to 50%.
DIAMETER	A straight line passing side-to-side through the middle of a circle.
EQUILATERAL TRIANGLE	A type of triangle. All sides and angles are of equal value. All angles are 60°.
ESTIMATION	A rough calculation or guess.
FACTOR	A factor is a number that can be divided wholly into another number. For example, 4 is a factor of 8.
FRACTIONS	A type of number, for example ½ is equivalent to a half.
FREQUENCY	The frequency of a specific data is the number of times that number occurs (Frequent).
HIGHEST COMMON FACTOR (HCF)	To find the HCF, you need to find all of the factors of two or more numbers, and then see which number is the highest.

IMPERIAL UNITS	Imperial units of length, mass and capacity. Includes inch, foot, yard, ounce, pound, stone, pint and gallon.
ISOSCELES TRIANGLE	A type of triangle. Two sides and angles are of the same value.
LOWEST COMMON MULTIPLE (LCM)	To find the LCM, you need to find all of the multiples of two or more numbers, and then work out the lowest number in common.
MEAN	A type of average. Add up all of the numbers and divide it by how many numbers there are.
MEDIAN	A type of average. Rearrange the numbers in ascending order. What number is in the middle?
METRIC UNITS	Metric units of length, mass and capacity. Includes mm, cm, km, mg, g, kg, ml and litres.
MODE	A type of average. What number occurs the most?
MULTIPLE	A multiple simply means 'times tables'. The multiples of 2 are 2, 4, 6, 8 and so on.
NEGATIVE NUMBER	A negative number is a number less than 0. On a scale, positive numbers move to the right, and negative numbers move to the left. Indicated by the sign '-'. For example, -4.
OBTUSE ANGLE	A type of angle. An obtuse angle is more than 90° but less than 180°.
PARALLEL LINE	A parallel line is two or more lines that are always the same distance apart, and never touch.
PERIMETER	A measurement of a surface. The line forming the boundary of a closed geometrical figure.
PERPENDICULAR LINES	A perpendicular line is two lines that meet at a right angle (90°).
PI	The mathematic constant 3.14159... The ratio of a circle's circumference to its diameter.

POSITIVE NUMBER	A positive number is a number more than 0. On a scale, positive numbers move to the right, and negative numbers move to the left.
PROBABILITY	The extent to whether something is likely to occur.
RADIUS	The radius is a straight line.
RANGE	A type of average. The range between the largest number and the smallest number.
RATIO	The quantitative relation between two amounts showing the number of times one value contain or is contained within the other.
REFLEX ANGLE	A type of angle. A reflex angle is more than 180° but less than 360°.
RIGHT-ANGLED TRIANGLE	A type of triangle. A triangle that has a 90° angle.
SCALENE TRIANGLE	A triangle with no equal angles or equal length sides.
SIGNIFICANT FIGURES	The digits carrying meaning. This allows us get a rough idea. For example, 48,739. The '4' is a significant figure because it represents 40 thousand.
SIMPLIFYING FRACTIONS	A way of making a fraction easier to read by finding a whole number that can be divided equally into both the denominator and numerator. For example, 12/24 can be simplified to 1/2. Both '12' and '24' can be divided by 12.
SQUARED NUMBER	A square number is the number that is reached when multiplying two of the same numbers together. For example 9 is the square number of 3 x 3.
SYMMETRY	Symmetry is when one shape becomes exactly like another if it's flipped or rotated.
VOLUME	The amount of space that a shape or object occupies. Contained within a container.

APPENDIX C

ALTERNATING CURRENT	An alternating current (AC) is a current that is continuously changing direction.
AMMETER	An ammeter is an electrical unit that measures current. An ammeter needs to be connected in series.
BATTERY	A battery supplies the electrical charge of a circuit. A battery contains more than one cell (see cell for definition)
BUZZER	A buzzer is a transducer which converts energy into sound.
CAPACITOR	A capacitor stores the electrical charge of the circuit. It can be used alongside a resistor in a 'timing' circuit. It acts as a sort of 'filter', whereby it blocks direct current (DC) signals, but permits alternating current (AC) signals from running through the circuit.
CELL	A cell is the component of a circuit that supplies the electrical charge. The larger terminal of the symbol represents the positive element and the smaller terminal represents the negative element. More than one cell = battery.
CLOSED SWITCH	A closed switch allows a current to flow through a circuit. This is done by closing the switch, which is what you would call an 'on switch', (i.e. it has the power to turn the circuit 'on').
CONDUCTOR	An electrical conductor is anything or any material which can carry an electrical current. Other conductors may conduct heat.
DIODE	A diode is an electrical device that only permits current flow in one direction.
DIRECT CURRENT	A direct current can be established if the current flows in one direction. For example, batteries and solar cells supply direct currents, with a typical battery supplying 1.5 V.

ELECTRON	A subatomic particle that carries the smallest of magnitudes of negative electricity.
FUSE	A fuse acts as a 'safety device' for electrical circuits. The fuse will blow i.e. melt, if the current flowing through the circuit exceeds a specified amount.
HEATER	A heater is a transducer that converts electrical energy into heat.
INDUCTOR	An inductor is an output device which includes a coil of wire that subsequently creates a magnetic field when a current passes through. It can often be used as a transducer to convert electrical energy into mechanical energy by this idea of 'pulling on something'.
INSULATOR	An insulator is a material which acts as a very poor conductor of electricity. Electrical wires are often covered with an insulating material in order to guard the circuit's electrical supply and provide a safety precaution to people using them.
LAMP	A lamp, or a bulb, is used as a transducer which converts the electrical energy within a circuit to permit light. This is often used within cars to indicate a warning light on the dashboard.
LIGHT DEPENDENT RESISTOR	A light dependent resistor, or a photoresistor, is a light-controlled variable. They change resistance as the light level changes.
LIGHT EMITTING DIODE	Often abbreviated as LED, light emitting diode is a transducer which converts energy into light.
OHMMETER	Ohmmeter is a unit that measures resistance.
OHM'S LAW	Ohm's law states that the current in a circuit between two points is directly proportional to the voltage and inversely proportional to resistance.

OPEN SWITCH	An open switch prevents a current to flow through the circuit.
RESISTOR	A resistor is a term that is quite self-explanatory. It restricts the flow of the current. For example, a resistor can be used to restrict the flow of current in an LED.
THERMISTOR	A thermistor is an input device relating to sensors. It is a transducer which converts temperature and heat, into resistance i.e. an electrical property.
TRANSFORMER	A transformer is a type of power supply. It contains two coils of wiring which is linked by an iron core. They are used to increase or decrease alternating current (AC) voltages. The transformer transfers energy through magnetic fields, not electrical fields.
VARIABLE RESISTOR	A variable resistor is used to control the current flow. This type of resistor contains 2 contacts. The resistor permits the control of adjusting lamp brightness and motoring speed.
VOLTMETER	A voltmeter is an electrical unit that measures voltage. This is also known as 'potential difference'.

APPENDIX D

AIR-INJECTION SYSTEM	An engine system that forces air into the exhaust system which burns fuels prior to coming out the exhaust pipe.
ALL-WHEEL DRIVE	All wheel drive, also known as four-wheel drive, is when all the wheels push and pull the car at the same time.
BRAKE SYSTEM	The system which consists of all the braking elements of a vehicle.
CATALYTICAL CONVERTER	Controls and oxidizes hydrocarbons and carbon monoxide into water vapour and carbon dioxide.
COMPRESSION	The reduction of fuel mixture in an internal combustion engine before ignition.
DISC BRAKES	Disc brakes are brakes which employ friction of pads against a disc attached to the wheel.
DRUM BRAKES	Drum brakes are brakes that use friction caused by pads pressing against a rotating brake drum.
EXHAUST	The exhaust system is piping used to guide reaction exhaust gases away from controlled combustion inside an engine.
EXHAUST-GAS-RECIRCULATION SYSTEM	A system which monitors and controls the nitrogen oxide emissions.
FRONT-WHEEL DRIVE	Front wheel drive is when the front wheels pull the car.
POSITIVE-CRANKCASE VENTILATION	An old strategy which forces unburned fuel back into the cylinder so that it can be burned.
OCTANE RATINGS	A number which indicates the anti-knock properties of fuel.
REAR-WHEEL DRIVE	Rear wheel drive is when the rear wheels pull the car.

THROTTLE	A valve located between the air intake filter and the intake manifold. It regulates the air which goes into the engine, based on the driver's input on the gas pedal.
TRANSMISSION	A transmission is a machine which provides power.

Take a look at our other technical guides

FOR MORE INFORMATION ON OUR TESTING GUIDES, PLEASE CHECK OUT THE FOLLOWING:

WWW.HOW2BECOME.COM

Get Access To
FREE
Reasoning
Test Questions

www.PsychometricTestsOnline.co.uk

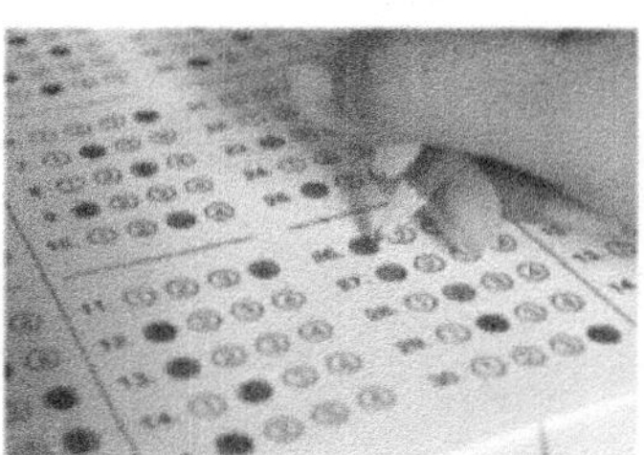

Printed and bound by CPI Group (UK) Ltd, Croydon, CR0 4YY

06/07/2026

02157571-0001